THE KENPEITAI IN JAVA AND SUMATRA

TRANSLATED BY
BARBARA GIFFORD SHIMER & GUY HOBBS

THE KENPEITAI IN JAVA AND SUMATRA

EQUINOX PUBLISHING (ASIA) PTE LTD
No 3. Shenton Way
#10-05 Shenton House
Singapore 068805

www.EquinoxPublishing.com

The Kenpeitai in Java and Sumatra
Translated by Barbara Gifford Shimer & Guy Hobbs

ISBN 978-602-8397-10-0

First Equinox Edition 2010

Copyright © 1986 by Cornell Southeast Asia Program Publications; renewed 2010. This edition is authorized by the original publisher, Cornell Southeast Asia Program Publications.

Printed in the United States

1 3 5 7 9 10 8 6 4 2

All rights reserved. No part of this publication may be reproduced, stored in a retrieval system, or transmitted in any form or by any means, electronic, mechanical, photocopying, recording or otherwise without the prior permission of Equinox Publishing.

TABLE OF CONTENTS

INTRODUCTION: HELLCRAFT, NOSTALGIA, AND ERROR
Thoughts on Memoirs of the Kenpeitai in Wartime Indonesia
by Theodore Friend 7

TRANSLATORS' PREFACE 17

SELECTIONS FROM THE AUTHENTIC HISTORY OF THE
KENPEITAI 25

    THE JAVA KENPEITAI 27
    THE SUMATRA KENPEITAI 55
    TERMINATION OF THE WAR AND THE JAVA
        KENPEITAI 69
    THE TWENTY-FIFTH ARMY KENPEITAI AND
        MAJOR GENERAL HIRANO 77
    THE SPECIFIC CHARACTER OF THE DUTCH
        WAR CRIMES TRIALS 81

BIBLIOGRAPHY 83

HELLCRAFT, NOSTALGIA, AND ERROR THOUGHTS ON MEMOIRS OF THE KENPEITAI IN WARTIME INDONESIA

THEODORE FRIEND

Who cares to understand the Kenpeitai? These memoirs[1] of the Japanese military police in the Second World War are collected for principals, friends, and sympathizers. They may therefore read strangely to people of other nations, and other persuasions. The writers, long after the events, lavishly distribute in-group credit for courage under duress and imagination in adversity. They highlight cases where individuals among them have understood native norms and brightened the lives of desolate and oppressed Indonesians. They find the Dutch-administered war crimes trials almost maniacally unjust.

War stories rarely rise to the level of literature. Generally they gratify the participants in particular. These are not exceptional, but they are welcome because until recently it was not readily possible to understand the Kenpeitai in Southeast Asia from their own point of view. Now it is possible. The record is filled in. At worst, however, it may remind us of

---

1 The surviving Kenpeitai have looked to their reputations with a recent trilogy. The basic work, of which the Java and Sumatra sections follow in translation, is Zenkoku Kenyūkai Rengōkai Hensan linkai [Editorial Committee of the National Federation of Kenpeitai Veterans' Associations], *Nihon Kenpei Seishi* [The Authentic History of the Kenpeitai] (Tokyo: Zenkoku Kenyūkai Rengōkai Honbu, 1976). A successor volume adds further details and lesser narrative accounts, while expanding on self-justifying themes: Zenkoku Kenyūkai Rengōkai Hensan linkai [Editorial Committee of the National Federation of Kenpeitai Veterans' Associations], *Nihon Kenpei Gaishi* [The General History of the Kenpeitai] (Tokyo, 1983). For the sake of brevity, the first will be referred to hereafter as the *Seishi,* and the second as the *Gaishi.* A companion volume will be referred to as the *Isho: Junkoku Kenpei no Isho [* Last Testaments of Kenpei Who Died for their Country] (Tokyo: Tokyo Kenyūkai and Zenkoku Kenyūkai Rengōkai (1982).

press reports of the Waffen SS in their annual reunion, rejoicing to the degree that President Reagan's 1985 visit to Bitburg might help to clear their reputation. The Kenpeitai have had no inadvertent American help, but presumably are cheered by the style of Premier Nakasone's recent visit to the Yasukuni Shrine.

Like the Waffen SS, and particularly its Death's Head Division (*Totenkopfverbände*),[2] the Kenpeitai were marked by extraordinary discipline and motivated by racial and political fanaticism. Like them they were a source of terror and repression to others, which fed a fierce sub-civilized pride in themselves. Although the Death's Head forces had originated as prewar guards of concentration camps and then expanded their functions to become one of the most effective units fighting the Russians, the Kenpeitai were rarely a field combat force except in counterespionage forays. Among other functions, they retained their predominant role as camp guards to the end.

If the Kenpeitai have less to apologize for than the Waffen SS, reputation-clearing is nonetheless a major motive in these tomes of 1500 and 1400 pages. Their writers, however, do not reach out imaginatively toward a global public. From the evidence here, former Kenpeitai officers expect little of world opinion. They appear confident of esteem only in the subculture of Japanese militaristic nationalism, vanquished in historic fact, but vindicable in memory. These, in sum, are memoirs that rejoice in events known to a few, and with a perspective that will not be shared by many.

That we have parts of the whole, in excellent English, is a result of the labors of Barbara Gifford Shimer and Guy Hobbs, Americans dedicated to command of the Japanese language, and to understanding of Japanese values. As assistants to me at the Woodrow Wilson International Center for Scholars, at the Smithsonian Institution Building in Washington, where I was a Fellow, 1983-84, they labored successfully to make the *Seishi* sections on Indonesia and the Philippines comprehensible to a wider range of scholars. Only the parts on Java and Sumatra are published here, buttressed by references to their sequels in the *Gaishi*, which Shimer has subsequently translated, and to the *Isho,* a collection of writings of the

---

[2] See, particularly, Charles W. Sydnor, *Soldiers of Destruction: The SS Death's Head Division, 1933-1945* (Princeton: Princeton University Press, 1977).

Kenpei facing death.

The Kenpeitai has not received the analysis in English that its German equivalents of World War II have received. One may not proceed with loose analogies in mind. The Kenpeitai were military police whose power had increased corresponding to the influence of the military and of the police in Japan in the 1930s, and at a geometrical rate because they combined both functions. In Japan the ordinary metropolitan police in that era could be brutal to those whom they saw as political deviants. Nishijima Shigetada, later a key figure in Japanese-Indonesian discussions during the surrender/independence crisis, was arrested three times as a Marxist in the 1930s, and the third time jailed for two years. He was tortured by suspension by a rope from the ceiling with his hands tied behind his back. During interrogation, a police tough jammed a hot iron in his behind, making him lurch forward in fright and pain at his interrogator, who hit him in the left eye, leaving him partially blinded.[3] If this were police treatment of their own nationals, what might be military police treatment of captured peoples suspected of subversion?

Overseas, in the Great Pacific War, the Kenpeitai commander reported directly to the Commander-in-Chief of the Army of the region—Sixteenth in Java, Twenty-fifth in Sumatra, Fourteenth in the Philippines. So did the commander of the Tokkōka, whose function was more specifically the Orweljian one of the "Thought Police." The Kenpeitai overlapped the Tokkōka to some degree, but their general responsibility is better described, in their own language, as "control and suppression." Their functions, more specifically, were investigation and punishment.

The Kenpeitai could investigate, and through a military court, even try and punish fellow military personnel. That accounts in part for their extraordinary power: a Kenpeitai officer might rebuke or arrest a regular army officer two or three ranks above him, and no one would readily interfere. And, although there may well be such instances, I have come across no case in which a regional commander in the Southern Army refused the recommendation or countermanded the initiative of the Kenpeitai.[4]

---

3 Nishijima interview, March 20, 1968.
4 Hesitations and reroutings might, of course, occur. The translation which follows contains the story of the offending director of the Palembang army hospital. It illustrates causes and

Such power among Japanese was incomparably multiplied, in wartime circumstances, among peoples the Japanese saw as "natives." Counterespionage was increasingly required for Japanese security as the war proceeded. Summary justice, the Kenpeitai's last resort, became more and more commonplace an expedient in the final two years of hostilities. Among the ordinary Japanese military, the Kenpeitai was often the tail that wagged the dog. Among conquered peoples, they were felt to be the bark and the bite of the Japanese Army. And if the ordinary citizen had a tendency to mythicize the Kenpeitai out of immediate fear, the Kenpeitai has a tendency to mythologize itself in nostalgic glory.

The spirit of the narratives that follow is best summed up, if a bit on the dire and dashing side, in the term *kikōsaku*. As a Kenpei code word, it meant severe punishment without martial law proceedings. That in turn meant execution. Ms. Shimer points out[5] that the term kikōsaku combines elements of Buddhist mythology with a sense of routine organizational mechanics. An apt English translation might be Operation Hades, which suggests both the nether world inhabited by the shades of the dead, and modern systematic effort, logistically rationalized. This, however, is not just one "operation" with a limited objective and a deadline. In fact, by kikōsaku, the Java Kenpeitai writer means, as he and his colleagues by usage intended, to describe summary justice—usually beheading without benefit of the defense counsel and evidentiary sortings out, which were customary in courts martial.

For an American or Australian scholar, say, to speak of courts martial, is already to have left one's most familiar context of "due process" and "presumption of innocence." To speak of a Japanese court martial is a long stride further away. Adding exigent wartime circumstances in a culture oblique to the Japanese makes justice as the Japanese then saw it harder still to envision. When we take the last step into kikōsaku, we have arrived at circumstances where investigator, prosecutor, judge, jury, and executioner are all from the same unit of police. Sometimes, under extreme duress, they could all presumably be the same person. To those

---

techniques of political delay and acceleration in the larger military-political system of which the military police was a part. The Kenpeitai prevailed in the end; justly, it would appear, in that instance.

5 Note 34 to the translation following.

accustomed to observing procedural niceties in English-derived law, such a condition is the very antithesis of justice.

There was no appeal for clemency provided for in the system of which kikōsaku was part. No civil official was going to take all things into consideration, including logically irrelevant but politically significant sympathies, and order a stay of execution, or even a pardon. The Kenpeitai commander might have to get the approval of the regional commander-in-chief before proceeding with an execution, or a batch of them. Indigenous political sensitivities apparently could sometimes delay implementation of a Kenpeitai verdict, or might conceivably soften it. But nothing was likely to change it except the Kenpeitai's own convenience, or its rarely changed convictions.

Delays, formalities, the Kenpeitai would sometimes put up with. Even they lived within a hierarchy: and seemliness is important within hierarchies, even when chaos announces itself as the usurping king. By using the term kikōsaku, however, with its netherworld connotations, the Japanese Kenpei seemed to appropriate the powers of hell to themselves. Let's get on with it, the term suggests. We know what has to be done, and we are equal to doing it. We will do it with dispatch, and dignity, and even by our standards, with aesthetic beauty. We will, in short, cut off a guilty head with a samurai sword, rather than waste weeks or months of valuable military time and energy, because the compelling idea that we serve—the Holy War for the Liberation of a Billion Asians—must be honored.

So, I suggest, a vernacular translation of kikōsaku might be "hellcraft." The Kenpeitai were hell's angels in their own minds: trained to fierce deeds swiftly determined. They stood proudly at the conjuncture of elevated ends and subterranean means. They were capable, they proudly felt, beyond the nerve of others. Looking back, they appear to themselves heroic in their hellcraft.

These are, it may be well to remember, the memoirs of captains and lieutenants and sergeants. Somewhere among them, by some lights, there may have been great souls; but these are certainly not the memoirs of statesmen. "This was what we faced," so the stories run. "This is how we solved it. This is how it was done. Now, long after, is come time to praise famous men. Is it true, in fact, that we are not famous, but infamous in the eyes of others? Then let us celebrate ourselves."

Those interested in the subject may be grateful that motives otherwise obscure have been by these narratives clarified, and that some light has been cast on historical moments that would be otherwise almost completely dark. There must be, nonetheless, some reservations in this gratitude. For the explanations in these memoirs also carry with them a certain amount of self-deception. And the effort at justification of past deeds sometimes staggers under the extra burden of self-glorification.

Two tales in particular are worth special comment. One is that of "Dr. Maruzuki," who is punished for allegedly sabotaging the Japanese war effort by poisoning volunteer laborers. The other is of the Islamic rebellion at Tasikmalaya early in 1945.

"Maruzuki" is not even close to the doctor's correct name. All the facts here presented suggest that the person in question was the distinguished bacteriologist and Director of the Eykman Institute, Professor Dr. Muchtar. He certainly did not kill hundreds of innocent fellow Javanese, as suggested in these memoirs.[6] Nothing in his character or past suggests that he could conceive of medical murder as a way to sabotage the Japanese conscript labor program, and hence their war effort.

The disease that struck the laborers in question was not dysentery, as stated here, but tetanus. The cause of the "epidemic" was most probably a batch of vaccine prepared under the responsibility of Japanese physicians at the Pasteur Institute, and inadvertently botched. The arrest of Indonesians became important to save face for the Japanese military physicians who would otherwise have been implicated.

Muchtar, summoned to treat the hundreds of victims, writhing and dying from contaminated vaccines, appears to have endangered himself by trying to unravel the cause of the situation. Questions were embarrassing. The investigator was arrested as the instigator. The threat to Japanese reputations was removed by identifying Indonesian scapegoats. Muchtar was imprisoned for nine months and executed on

---

6 Sukarno in his own memoirs, *Sukarno: An Autobiography as told to Cindy Adams* (Indianapolis: Bobbs-Merrill, 1965), pp. 193-94, goes even further than the *Seishi*, and speaks of "tens of thousands" dying in three days from "faulty vaccine." Because of the "enormity" of what (Sukarno assumed) Muchtar had done, he told medical students at the time that he could not intervene. Sukarno continued, in short, to believe the Kenpeitai version until his own death in 1970. Abu Hanifah, *Tales of Revolution* (Sydney: Angus and Robertson, 1972), pp. 125-27, gives a devastating refutation of Sukarno's version.

July 8, 1945. Two colleagues of his were not executed, but died of torture and starvation.[7]

The story as related through Kenpei memories, however, is a travesty of misinformation and obfuscation, concluding in the absurd misstatement that the offender's "punishment was relatively light." The Japanese not only beheaded Muchtar, but ran over his body with a steam roller and trucked the remains to a mass grave.[8] The Japanese medicine man who was actually in charge of the laboratory and responsible for the lethal vaccine was never, to my knowledge, apprehended or charged with any crime. The range of his culpability might run from criminal incompetence to diabolical experimentation, with the former more probable.[9]

In comparison with the Muchtar story, which shows Kenpeitai "investigation" at its shabbiest, and face saving at its cruelest, the Kenpeitai account of the Tasikmalaya revolt is a bit more elevated. This rendering reveals Japanese psychology about Islam, communism, and uprisings in general. Of the first they were wary. The second had to be prevented. The third had to be crushed.

The description of what happened at Tasikmalaya is perhaps the most concrete Japanese version of an event more renowned than researched. The writer's likening of the uprising to the "Ikko ikki" of late sixteenth century Kyoto is illuminating because that was a major threat to the sovereignty of the Tokugawa Shogunate. The element of outraged peasant sentiment occurs in both cases, although the noun "peasant" may hide a great variety of personal profiles and interests. In both cases religious zeal is critical: Shinshū Buddhist in the one instance, orthodox Muslim in the other. Kyai Zainal Mustafa, a revered traditionalist in the eyes of his followers, was a dangerous fanatic in the eyes of the Kenpeitai. Surviving the slaughter at the mosque, there was only one imaginable fate for him— summary court martial proceedings, and execution.

---

7 In a book-length manuscript being prepared for publication, I offer a fuller account of the incident, based on interviews with Dr. Bahder Djohan and Dr. Slamet Imam Santoso, and on documents in the Indische Collectie, Rijksinstituut voor Oorlogsdocumentatie, Amsterdam.
8 Abu Hanifah, *Tales of Revolution*, p. 127.
9 The case awakens memories of the Hygienic Institute of the Waffen SS, whose typhus experiments at Buchenwald, 1942-43, led to nearly 600 deaths (on which see Sydnor, *Soldiers of Destruction*, p. 339). Although there is evidence of similar Japanese experimentation in other theatres, the circumstances regarding *rōmusha* deaths by tetanus convey shocked and embarrassed surprise rather than conscious plan.

Recollection of the event spins the writer toward reflection on religious fanaticism from a Buddhist point of view. As he regards Islam, he stresses blind belief in fatalistic accord with the wish of Allah, and the difficulties of the Kenpeitai in dealing with the aftermath of their bloody victory at the mosque.

He is then led to reflections on communism, and appreciation of the fact that the Dutch had crushed the party, and its ideological infection, in 1927. The easy mental transition from rabid Islam to radical Marxism was commonplace in the Kenpeitai. They suspected Mohd. Hatta, for instance, on both accounts. His being devout in the one manner, speculative in the other, and an ornery independent in style, led to a Kenpeitai plot to assassinate him. It failed. Naturally enough, neither that plot nor its foiling is disclosed here.[10] In the Philippine section of this same volume, however, much is made of the investigative powers of the Kenpeitai in tracking down and eliminating the man who attempted to assassinate Jose P. Laurel, whom the Japanese had chosen for leadership of their occupation government. The wrong man, it turned out later: but they still do not realize it.[11]

Inheriting as they did—by Dutch design, some say, although that is difficult to prove—the files of the Netherlands Indies political police, the Kenpeitai may have been influenced by the sheer assiduous volume of Dutch investigatory prowess. That influence was all the more potent, mixed as it was with the aversions to strange religions and to Marxist creed, which were characteristic of militant Japanese nationalism.[12] Belief

---

10 I am preparing an account based on interviews with Miyoshi Shunkichirō, Yamamoto Moichiro, and Hatta himself.

11 The Kenpeitai believed that one Jirano Marcelino had led the plot. They tracked him down and he was shot by other military guards. The Kenpeitai were sorry to lose him that way, but were glad to have captured and dealt with his alleged co-conspirators by summary court martial, "and thereby preserve the dignity of the Kenpeitai." *(Nihon Kenpei Seishl*, Philippine Section, pp. 927-28 of Japanese original; quotation from Shimer/Hobbs translation, p. 21 (Japanese original p. 928). After the war, both the Hunters ROTC and the Markings guerrillas took credit for the attempted assassination. President Laurel thought he had identified the gunman, but did not prosecute him. None of those claims and clues appear to dovetail with the Kenpeitai investigation and executions.

12 Germaine A. Hoston, in an excellent series of articles, is illuminating the special perspectives of those prewar Japanese who melded their Marxism with indigenous, including nationalistic and even imperialistic, values: "Marxism and National Socialism in Taishō Japan: The Thought of Takabatake Motoyuki" *(Journal of Asian Studies,* 44, 1 [November 1984]: 43-64); "Marxism and Japanese Expressionism: Takahashi Kamekichi and the Theory of 'Petty Imperialism'" *[Journal*

in the Emperor, the quasi-magical polity *[kokutai]*, and the Greater East Asia Co-Prosperity Sphere were blended in a nativistic-imperial teleology that left no comfortable room for any other system of belief or cause of action.

The parallel of Kenpeitai suspicion with the Dutch police in anti-Islamic, anti-Marxist currents was, however, only a loose affinity of colonial consciousness. A deeper feeling among the Kenpeitai in Indonesia was competition with the Dutch. Military triumph had to be followed by effective psychological displacement of their imperial predecessors. This Japanese writer on Java does not quite bring it off. The Dutch penetrate the narrative as having ingeniously extracted the loyalty of "half-breeds" *(konketsu),* while exacting intellectual, economic, and, for that matter, political, poverty among the "natives." These almost incomprehensible "half-breeds" were held accountable for most of the danger faced by the Kenpeitai, who themselves were, in their own view, simple men who "sought only to maintain peace and protect the army."

The writer concludes that Dutch spying stratagems, by using half-breeds and excessively harassing the Kenpeitai, were the real cause of kikōsaku. The principal responsibility for criminal arrests and summary executions lies with the Dutch, who instigated those espionage activities in which many native lives were sacrificed. The war crimes trials therefore are not only an expression of Dutch vengeance, but an unjust reversal of fault. Such was the considered opinion of the Editorial Committee of the National Federation of Kenpeitai Veterans' Association in 1976. By 1983, that opinion had become still more pronounced in the *Gaishi*, which treats Dutch "hatred" for and "reprisal" upon the Kenpeitai for having "caused the breakdown of their colonial policy spanning three hundred years."[13]

---

of Japanese Studies, 10, 1 [1984]: 1-30); "Emperor, Nation, and the Transformation of Marxism to National Socialism in Prewar Japan: The Case of Sano Manobu" (*Studies in Comparative Communism,* 18, 1 [Spring 1985]). However important such indigenous syntheses of Marxism were to some Japanese theorists, they themselves, in the light of prevailing norms, were suspect of alien frailty or stark disloyalty. As for what Marxist activists might suffer, see the passage on Nishijima Shigetada, text above.

13 *Gaishi,* quotation from Shimer translation, p. 52 (page 1147 in Japanese original); see also Shimer translation, pp. 54-57, 61 (pages 1154-57 and 1159 of Japanese original). In a similar spirit is Yamazaki Toyoko's novel, *Two Fatherlands;* the central figure is a Nisei who is released from a wartime detention center for Japanese-Americans, to work for US Army Intelligence. He goes on

Such a perspective need not be shared by anyone else. Who behaved worse—the Dutch and the Americans in their original imperial conquests, or the Japanese, seeking to displace and succeed Western empires? Which was more unjust—kikōsaku enacted in the heat of war by temporary conquerors under conditions of extreme jeopardy, or war crimes trials as a "revenge of pride" perpetrated in the cool of peace by the eventual victors? These are questions which ramify in diffuse ways. But they are not maximally fertile as modes of inquiry.

Here, in any event, translated for a readership that the authors did not contemplate as they wrote, are the memoirs of the Kenpeitai units in Java and Sumatra. They are vastly more self-justifying than apologetic. How much of their vindicating tone should be conceded as a normal human tendency? Self-preservation is no doubt closer to the fundamentals of nature than self-criticism. Elementary canons of scholarship, nevertheless, make one restless with these narratives, without there being space to detail all the errors which they contain. With or without error, their combination of repression, atrocity, and pride makes them sources analogous to those of other unhappy histories, Americans in Batangas and Samar at the turn of the century, and the Dutch in Aceh.[14] A major difference, however, is that both North Atlantic powers faced bitter struggles to complete their conquests. That the Japanese behaved as detailed here, after easily capturing Indonesia in nine days, suggests what might have been the character of their empire had they succeeded in their "Holy War."

---

to serve as an interpreter at the Tokyo war crimes trials (1946-48), but disillusioned at the end by what he considers "victors' justice," he commits suicide. Beginning in 1981 and overlapping with US Congressional Hearings on compensation for wartime internees, Yamazaki's work was weekly serialized in Japan. When published as a novel in 1983 (the same year as the *Gaishi*), it sold almost one million copies.

14 Stuart Creighton Miller, *"Benevolent Assimilation," The American Conquest of the Philippines, 1899-1903* (New Haven: Yale University Press, 1982); Paul van't Veer, *De Atjeh-oorlog* (Amsterdam: Uitgeverij De Arbeiderspers, 1969).

TRANSLATORS' PREFACE

To understand the tone of recent Kenpei recollections, it helps to recall that in the final days of World War II, the Kenpeitai command bitterly opposed any Japanese proposals for surrender.[1] When the Emperor finally did concede defeat, some Kenpei squad leaders in the field refused to comply and fled to the hills to resist.[2] Once a complete Allied victory looked certain, the Kenpeitai burned many of its files in a frantic effort to conceal its war-time record.[3] These memoirs,[4] then, are significant first in that historians have few primary materials on the subject of the Kenpeitai in World War II. They are also important because they reveal the thinking of men who helped to shape some of the events of the Pacific War, and certainly helped determine the atmosphere under the Japanese occupation. Of more interest here than accounts of the historical facts, which are often inaccurate, are the tone and attitude of these veterans of the Kenpeitai. Their white-washing and self-vindication do not arise from having been written during the bitterness of the early postwar years, but from a new Japanese pride and nationalism of the last decade.

Historically considered, the Kenpeitai itself was part of a full-scale program of suppression, engineered by the Meiji oligarchs to contain forces potentially destabilizing to their emerging modern state. Created in 1881 with an elite corps of 349 men, the Kenpeitai first disciplined army

---

1 Lester Brooks, *Behind Japan's Surrender: The Secret Struggle that Ended an Empire* (New York: McGraw-Hill, 1968), p. 238.
2 *Gaishi*, p. 1147.
3 Interview with Dr. Akira Fujiwara, Hitotsubashi University, Tokyo, June 1985. On instructions to destroy records issued by the Japanese Ministry of War, see Records of the Office of the Provost Marshall General (RG 389), National Archives, Prisoner of War Operations Division, Information Bureau, Subject File, 1942-45, File: Japanese POW Information Bureau, S. Iguchi, "Report on the Destruction of Records and Documents of the Prisoner of War Information Bureau."
4 See footnote 1 of Dr. Friend's essay (above p. 1) for a complete citation.

officers who resisted the newly imposed requirement of conscription.[5] The officers—former samurai recently deprived of their military monopoly—loathed the idea of commanding an army of mere commoner troops.[6] The Kenpeitai also policed the growing unrest among the farmers and merchants newly subject to conscription. From the beginning, then, the Kenpeitai's duties were twofold: to police the army and to police the people.[7]

Since 1911, a separate corps, the Tokkō, had directed the campaign against exponents of subversive ideologies.[8] In the mid-1920s, the Kenpeitai joined forces and officially established its own Tokkō division, although it had in fact been jnvolved in anti-ideological work since 1881.[9] Increasingly in the Shōwa era, the Kenpeitai's targets were workers, students, farmers, socialists, and Communists. It stifled groups espousing foreign ideologies, pacifist sentiments, or irreverence for the Emperor. Its methods were designed to spread terror in the populace. The Kenpeitai extracted confessions and recantations through intimidation and abuse and, in a few instances, killed its prisoners.[10] By 1945, the Kenpeitai had arrested, detained, tortured, and imprisoned tens of thousands of Japanese.[11]

Overseas, the Kenpeitai was active in all of Japan's wars and occupied territories, including Formosa (1895-1945), Korea (1896-1945), and China (1901-1945), and during World War II in Burma, French Indo-China, Malaysia, the Philippines, and Indonesia. In the occupied territories, the

---

5 *Seishi*, p. 35, Ōtani Keijiro, *Shōwa Kenpei-shi* (Tokyo: Misuzu Shobō, 1979), pp. 4-5.
6 *Seishi*, p. 1380; Paul Akamatsu, *Meiji 1868: Revolution and Counter-Revolution in Japan* (New York: Harper and Row, 1972), p. 257.
7 Ōtani Keijiro, *Shōwa Kenpei-shi* , p. 5.
8 'Tokkō' is an acronym for Tokubetsu Kōtō Keisatsu [Special Higher Police], also called "thought control police." It had a predecessor named Koto Keisatsu [Higher Police], organized in 1904. Richard H. Mitchell, *Thought Control in Prewar Japan* (Ithaca: Cornell University Press, 1976), p. 25.
9 *Seishi*, pp. 370-71. A document describing in detail the workings of the Kenpeitai Tokkō, prepared by Kenpeitai Second Division Commander Colonel Noguchi Masao for General MacArthur, is reproduced in full in Gaishi, pp. 1304-14.
10 In 1923 when the massive earthquake hit Tokyo, the Kenpeitai took the opportunity of the ensuing chaos to kill Osugi Sakae, the Japanese anarchist, by strangulation. John W. Dower, *Origins of the Modern Japanese State: Selected Writings of E. H. Norman* (New York: Pantheon, 1975), pp. 58, 355. Also on that day, the metropolitan police imprisoned or killed Koreans and alleged extremists. Ienaga Saburo, *The Pacific War: World War II and the Japanese, 1931-1945* (New York: Pantheon, 1978), pp. 8, 60.
11 Brooks, *Behind Japan's Surrender*, p. 237.

Kenpeitai maintained order among the indigenous peoples and sought to crush any form of anti-Japanese mobilization. It censored the press, monitored suspected subversives, eradicated networks of spies, and maintained an undercover surveillance of post offices, railway stations, hotels, schools, temples, and other public gathering places. For disobedient civilians, it meted out punishments that were swift and harsh.[12]

During World War II, the worst Kenpei excesses occurred in prisoner-of-war and civilian internment camps. These held captured Allied soldiers and civilian European colonialists, respectively. Conditions in many camps were appalling. Prisoners were kept in filth and squalor in overcrowded pens with inadequate food and water. Starved, exhausted, and diseased, they were made to work day and night, and beaten repeatedly, often at random.[13] The Kenpeitai also went to great lengths to contrive tortures of a most depraved nature.[14]

On November 1, 1945, in one of his first acts, General Douglas MacArthur disbanded the Kenpeitai, which by then had grown to a force of 36,000 men stationed overseas and in Japan. In 1952, the year the occupation ended, former Kenpei in Tokyo, Osaka, and other cities formed local Kenpeitai Veterans' Associations. On March 21, 1953, the separate local chapters formed an umbrella organization, the Zenkoku Kenyūkai Rengōkai (National Federation of Kenpeitai Veterans' Associations). The Zenkenren (its acronym) prides itself on being the "leading war veterans' group in Japan, with the strongest organization and best esprit de corps."[15]

---

12 *Seishi*, pp. 9-28; *Gaishi*, p. 1155; George S. Kanahele, "The Japanese Occupation of Indonesia: Prelude to Independence," (Ph.D. dissertation, Cornell University, 1967), p. 259, n. 70.

13 On prisoner-of-war camps in Java and Sumatra, see Doetje van Velden, *De Japanse interneringskampen voor burgers gedurende de Tweede Wereldoorlog* (Franeker: Wever, 1977), and Records of the Office of the Provost Marshall General (RG 389), National Archives, Prisoner of War Operations Division, Information Bureau, Subject File, 1942-45.

14 Edward F.L. Russell, *The Knights of Bushido: The Shocking History of Japanese War Atrocities* (New York: Dutton, 1958), pp. 274 ff. This book contains a complete catalogue of tortures employed by the Kenpeitai, including first person accounts by survivors of specific instances in Java and Sumatra. Some methods clearly go far beyond the infliction of pain for the delimited purposes of extracting information or punishing a violation of camp rules. Forcing water from a hose down a victim's throat and nose, then jumping on his bloated stomach; making prisoners stand for days at a stretch crammed in a tight cage of barbed wire set on top of a nest of red ants; lashing a dehydrated man with barbed wire to the trunk of a tree without water for two days and placing a bucket of water right in front of his eyes—these are deeds conceived and committed by the Kenpeitai.

15 *Gaishi*, p. 1397.

As of June 1985, membership was 4,000 representing one third of the former Kenpei alive today.[16]

The four stated goals of the Zenkenren are to "affirm the value of the Kenpeitai"; to honor Kenpei war dead; to promote comradery; and to aid the families of those lost in the war.[17] In 1969, the Zenkenren erected a small memorial to the Kenpei war dead in a quiet corner on the grounds of Yasukuni Jinja, a famous Shinto shrine in Tokyo which memorializes the legions of Japan's war dead.[18] Funds for the memorial came from Zenkenren members, their families, and friends. Japanese people ostracized Kenpeitai veterans after the war, and thus to have a memorial so near the revered Yasukuni Jinja serves to enhance Kenpei standing, at least in their own eyes. "Just about no one knows about it," brood the authors of *Seishi*, "the Kenpei memorial stands quietly deep in the woods of Yasukuni, glistening under the great shrine gates. But that is all that can be expected. For the Kenpei memorial harbors a spirit which only the Kenpei can understand."[19]

To promote comradery among its members, the Zenkenren publishes a quarterly magazine called *Kenyū* [Kenpeitai Comrades]. The April 1985 edition, which can be taken to be typical, carries a review of an article in the Japanese press about the Nanking massacre of 1937. An editorial discusses what it calls President Reagan's second American revolution. There is also an imaginary letter from a Kenpei youth who died in the war, followed by his friend's reply. We can see group portraits of local Kenpei reunions held in restaurants and public parks. There is an advertisement for a Kenpei figurine in uniform, enclosed in a glass case suitable for display in the home.

To the Zenkenren, the *Seishi*, *Gaishi*, and *Isho* constitute the definitive trilogy of Kenpeitai history.[20] These vast and sometimes rambling memoirs were written by an editorial board of sixty members appointed from the

---

16 Interview in Tokyo with Mr. Yoshida Nisaku, former Kenpeitai squad commander in Changzhou, China and current president of the TōkōPrinting Co., publisher of the *Seishi, Gaishi, Isho*, and other Kenyūkai publications, June 1985.

17 *Isho*, p. 631. Neither pensions nor other government assistance provides for the families of Kenpei war dead. Interview with Yoshida Nisaku, June 1985.

18 In Japan, it plays a role analogous to that of the Tomb of the Unknown Soldier in the United States. Edwin O. Reischauer, *The Japanese* (Cambridge: Harvard University Press, 1977), p. 219.

19 *Seishi*, p. 1320.

20 *Isho*, p. 7.

Zenkenren. Each editor took responsibility for a part of the manuscript, and together they solicited diaries, letters, and reminiscences from over a thousand former Kenpei. The Zenkenren commissioned Mr. Ashizawa Norio, a non-Kenpei author, to edit the *Seishi*, and he worked closely with the Kenpei editors of each section.[21] The Zenkenren followed the same procedure in producing the *Gaishi*, and collaborated with the Tokyo Kenyūkai in its production of the *Isho*. The *Seishi* (published in 1976) took five years to compile; the *Gaishi* and *Isho* (published in 1983 and 1982, respectively) took two years each.[22] The *Seishi* has sold 7,000 copies; the *Gaishi*, 3,500 copies; and the *Isho*, 2,300 copies.[23]

The *Seishi* is organized chronologically, with sections entitled "Meiji and Taishō" (1868-1925), "Shōwa Upheaval" (1926-36), "War-torn Shōwa" (1937-45), and "The Termination of the War and the War Crimes Trials." The selections translated here are the Java and Sumatra chapters found in both "War-torn Shōwa" and "The Termination of the War and the War Crimes Trials." The *Gaishi* is organized geographically, with sections on Japan, Manchuria, China, the Philippines, Malaysia, Burma, French Indo-China, and Indonesia. It ends with a section entitled "The Termination of the War," which includes recollections of prisoner-of-war camps and the war crimes trials. The *Isho* is a collection of last testaments by Kenpei who committed suicide or received the death sentence. Many were written in the last hours of life. Among the 300 or so pieces, we find letters to mothers and fathers, messages for friends and lovers, and inner thoughts on Kenpei destinies. Many of the poems display a finesse in the use of the Japanese language. Directly after receiving the sentence of death by firing squad, a captain from Java writes, "Oh, the joys and worries of life are gone, and with them I fade too. Yearning for my mother and father."[24]

A major, also from Java, who elsewhere says that world peace would bring him supreme joy, writes, "Momentarily my life draws to a close, but there is not a cloud in the sky over Japan. Now, my skin feels cold again.

---

21 Interview with Mr. Yoshida Nisaku, Tokyo, July 1985.
22 *Gaishi*, p. 1397; *Isho*, p. 632.
23 *Kenyū*, p. 3. Interview with Mr. Yoshida Nisaku, president of the Toko Printing Co., in June 1985.
24 Captain Sato, "Last Testament in Verse," *Isho*, p. 407.

The drone of the mosquito—it is my death knell."²⁵

It is revealing to compare the tone of the *Seishi* published nine years ago, with that of the *Gaishi* and *Isho,* published only two and three years ago, respectively. The theme of self-justification is stronger in the latter, and the authors apparently feel less guilt for the means they used to achieve their ends. More than the *Seishi,* the chapters on Java and Sumatra in the *Gaishi* paint a rosy picture of Kenpeitai relations with the indigenous Indonesians and the immigrant Chinese. In the *Gaishi,* the authors try hard to convince the reader of the Kenpeitai's professed support for the Indonesian independence movement. Also, the *Gaishi* is more openly cynical about the integrity of the Dutch war crimes trials.²⁶ It more readily admits that torture was used on "terrorists and spies," but is quick to justify its use.²⁷ Furthermore, the latter works have a more selfassured tone, and this reflects a general trend in Japanese historiography toward revisionism on the subject of World War II. Paralleling this trend, public opinion regarding the Kenpeitai has improved somewhat in recent years, in the view of members of the Zenkenren.²⁸ Finally, whereas the *Seishi*

---

25 Nonaka Takami, "Last Testament in Verse," *Isho,* pp. 397-98.
26 *Gaishi,* pp. 1111-12, 1154-60.
27 See *Gaishi,* pp. 1115, 1156.
28 Interview in June 1985 with Satoru Ōnishi, former Kenpeitai major and Tokkō captain, a major member of the *Seishi* editorial committee.

Two sources which have influenced public opinion about the Kenpeitai bear mentioning. One is Nakazawa Keiji's *Hadashi no Gen* [Barefoot Gen] (Tokyo: Chōbunsha, 1975, 42nd printing: July 1985), a nine volume comic which seriously treats the events before and after the atomic bombing of Hiroshima. The comic is considered a long seller (2.8 million sold), is nationally recognized, and is often assigned to middle and high school students for summer reading. Telephone interview with Chōbunsha, August 9, 1985. In the comic the Kenpeitai is portrayed as a brutal and dreaded corps. The comic is clearly anti-war, as is evident from illustrations of anti-military protest, the Tokkō deserter, and the fate of conscript Korean and Chinese. The second source is Fukada Yūsuke, *Ennetsu Shōnin* [Zealous Merchants], (Tokyo: Bungeishunju, 1982) 523 pp., a best seller and winner of the Naoki-shō, the most esteemed award for popular literature. Produced for television, it was broadcast on NHK three times, consecutively capturing a 15 percent (one million) audience share. Bungeishunju, NHK telephone interview, August 9, 1985. Written from the viewpoint of a Japanese-Filipino, the book tells the stories of Kenpeitai Captain Baba in the Japanese-occupied Philippines in the 1940s, and a Japanese trading company Manila branch chief Kodera in the 1970s. Kenpeitai Captain Baba is portrayed as a martyr who saves his Filipina lover, local residents, and fellow Kenpeitai by driving a truck of explosives into approaching United States troops. The author draws a clear parallel between the Captain and the Japanese executive Kodera, who is killed by exploited Filipino laborers. Both are portrayed as humanists, pro-Filipino, martyrs, and pawns in a greater military and economic game. The story is based on an actual incident that took place in Manila in 1971, in which Filipino laborers shot three Japanese businessmen, killing one. All other events and characters in the book are fictional.

foresees no end to the world's hostility toward the Kenpeitai, the *Gaishi* and *Isho* expect that the story of the Kenpeitai will at least reinstill a sense of patriotism in today's Japanese youth. The latter authors believe that the Kenpei who died by execution and suicide should be remembered not as war criminals but as valiant martyrs who died for the glory of Japan. The preface to the *Isho,* for example, promises the "unparalleled, noble, heart-felt messages[29] of patriots that have been left to the young people of the new generation by Kenpei who...were the victims of unjustified punishments and were thus the breakwater for a nation of a hundred million."[30]

In the war crimes trials, the Kenpeitai fared far worse than the Japanese army. For example, in the Batavia trials, from a pool of 20,000 regular army troops and only 538 Kenpei both stationed in Java at the end of the war, there were 58 convictions for regular troops as against 199 for Kenpei. Of these 199 Kenpei, 40 men received the death sentence. In Sumatra at the Medan trials, of 55 convicted Kenpei, 12 men received the death sentence.[31] Whatever one thinks of the judicial atmosphere and processes, a branch of the military in which well over a third of the men were convicted as war criminals requires historical understanding.

* * * * * * * *

In translating these memoirs, we faced the perennial dilemma of a literal versus a liberal translation. While trying to remain faithful line by line to the text, we have had to edit for the sake of readability in English. Japanese personal names appear as in the original—surnames first, given names second. Where multiple readings were possible for a Japanese name, we chose the most common reading for that name.[32] Where the spelling of a Dutch or Indonesian name was unclear from the transliterated Japanese rōmaji, we attempted a phonetic approximation of the Dutch or

---

29 Messēji in *rōmaji.*
30 *Isho,* preface by Iizuka Ken, pp. 5-8; Like sentiments appear in *Gaishi,* preface by Moriyasu Seiichi, pp. 11-13; *Seishi,* p. 1321.
31 *Seishi,* p. 1323; *Isho,* pp. 580-84.
32 As listed in P. G. O'Neill, *Japanese Names: A Comprehensive Index of Characters and Readings* (New York and Tokyo: Weatherhill, 1972).

Indonesian, and noted the rōmaji. We alone are responsible for any errors in the preface, translation, and notes.

Several people assisted us in our efforts to research this unexplored topic. We thank Dr. Imai Yoshio, currently of the Hoover Institution and former Fellow at the Woodrow Wilson International Center for Scholars, for sharing his knowledge. He also introduced us to Dr. Fujiwara Akira, professor of military history at Hitotsubashi University, whose comments and insights were very helpful. We are grateful to Dr. Kataoka Tetsuya, currently of the Hoover Institution and former Fellow at the Wilson Center, for providing advice on some of the more obscure passages of the Japanese text. We thank Mr. Philip Nagao of the Library of Congress in Washington, and Mr. Chiyo Masaaki of the National Diet Library in Tokyo for assistance in assembling a bibliography. For their interviews with Guy Hobbs, we are indebted to Mr. Yoshida Nisaku, Mr. Ōnishi Satoru, and Mr. Iizuka Kinjiro. Mr. Yoshida is a former Kenpertai Captain in Changzhou, China and current president of the Tōkō Printing Co., publisher of the *Seishi*, *Gaishi*, and *Isho*. Mr. Ōnishi, former Kenpeitai major and Tokkō captain on the Malay peninsula, was a principal member of the *Seishi* editorial committee, and is the author of *Hiroku Jōnan Kakyō Shukusei Jiken* [The Secret Record of the Singaporean Chinese: The Purge Incident]. Mr. Iizuka was a Kenpeitai Tokkō captain in Java from April 1942 to August 1945, and edited the Java section of the *Seishi*. We are especially grateful to Dr. Sadako Taylor who read the draft of the translation and contributed valuable criticism and comments. We also want to thank Bill Shimer for his help in the editing of the preface. Most of all, we are grateful to Dr. Theodore Friend, who by his guidance and encouragement brought us closer to an appreciation of the processes of history.

Selections from

THE AUTHENTIC HISTORY OF THE JAPANESE KENPEITAI

(NIHON KENPEI SEISHI)

by the

NATIONAL FEDERATION OF
KENPEITAI VETERANS' ASSOCIATIONS
(ZENKOKU KENYŪKAI RENGŌKAI HENSAN IINKAI)
TOKYO, 1976

[1025] THE JAVA KENPEITAI

The Third Field Kenpeitai

On July 16, 1941 the Third Field Kenpeitai was formed out of the Guandong Kenpeitai Training Regiment in Xinjing,[1] Manchukuo as follows:

Third Field Kenpeitai Commandant—Kenpei Colonel Kuzumi Kenzaburō
Vice Commander—Kenpei Captain Takayabu Saichirō
Attached Commissioned Officer[2]—Kenpei Major Ikeyama Yasushi:
    20 commissioned officers
First Company—Company Commander Kenpei Captain Yajima Shichisaburō:
    60 men
Second Company—Company Commander Kenpei Captain Kobayashi Shōkichi:
    60 men
Third Company—Company Commander Kenpei Captain Sugō Shūzō:
    60 men
Fourth Company—Company Commander Kenpei Captain Taniguchi Kiyoshi:
    60 men[3]

---

1 Xinjing was the capital of Manchukuo during the Japanese occupation. Now called Changchun, it is the capital of Jilin province in China.
2 Major Ikeyama Yasushi was the chief of the Kenpeitai Tokkō in Java. *Gaishi*, p. 1110.
3 These numbers total 262 Kenpei. In 1944, the Java Kenpeitai grew to 522. For 1945, there are conflicting estimates for the number of Kenpei in Java. The Japanese government statistic is 538 (*Seishi*, p. 1381). The *Gaishi* mentions that there were 800 by the end of the war; but this

On August 2, 1941, after reaching full strength, the Third Field Kenpeitai moved from Xinjing to Xinglongzhen on the outskirts of Mudanjiang,[4] where it was stationed to undergo in-service training. The training consisted primarily of individual squad combat drills of the type used in anti-Soviet operations, with special emphasis on gruelling anti-gas drills using actual poison gas that simulated real warfare.

The Greater East Asia War broke out on December 8, 1941 and on January 3, 1942 the Third Field Kenpeitai was ordered to mobilize. The Third Field Kenpeitai left its station in Mudanjiang on January 6, and arrived in Dalian on January 15. In Dalian the unit received supplementary men and officers, before setting sail on January 22, 1942.

From the day of its departure from Dalian, the Third Field Kenpeitai officially joined the ranks of the Sixteenth Army commanded by Lieutenant General Imamura Hitoshi. Aboard ship on the way to Gaoxiong Bay in Taiwan, we Kenpei received intensive instruction in the Malay language and other training appropriate to the southern regions.[5]

Subsequently the Third Field Kenpeitai joined the Sixteenth Army in the port of Cam Ranh in French Indo-China. By this time the Sixteenth Army had shifted its orientation to the advance on Java.[6]

The main strength of the Sixteenth Army landed in Banten Bay in west Java after the Surabaya and Batavia offshore naval battles, just before dawn on March first. The Batavia naval battle had erupted just after midnight early the same day when a fleet of our Japanese transports

---

figure undoubtedly includes Indonesian "auxiliary Kenpei" trained to assist the Japanese Kenpei. *(Gaishi,* p. 1125). In an interview with George Kanahele, former Kenpei Major Iizuka Kinjirō said there were close to 1,000 Kenpei in Java by 1945. This estimate probably also includes auxiliary Kenpei. Kanahele, "Japanese Occupation of Indonesia," p. 272, n. 52.

4 Mudanjiang (Botankō in Japanese) was the former military capital for the Japanese Guandong army. It is now a major city in Heilongjiang province, China. Xinglongzhen was a local administrative unit on the outskirts of Mudanjiang.

5 Many of the Third Field Kenpei who ended up in Java had studied the Russian language as part of their training for anti-Soviet warfare in Manchuria. With only a brief course aboard ship in Bahasa Indonesia, they were ill-prepared to communicate with the Indonesians. In fact, there was only one man in the Japanese military who was known by the Indonesians to speak their language fluently. (Kanahele, "Japanese Occupation of Indonesia," pp. 257; 273, n. 52.) In *Gaishi,* the authors acknowledge that many Kenpei did not take their assignment to learn Indonesian seriously. In fact, the Kenpei blame their ignorance of the native language for their arrest and punishment of innocent people. *(Gaishi,* p. 1115).

6 Upon hearing that Singapore had fallen to the Japanese on February 15, the Sixteenth Army headed south towards Java earlier than it had originally planned *(Gaishi,* p. 1109).

anchored in Banten Bay was attacked by the enemy. During the ensuing battle the two enemy ships from Australia and the US and our escort fleet confronted each other at point blank range.[7] One of our transports was sunk by a torpedo, and three ships were damaged when they ran aground. Fortunately our ships were in shallow waters because we had come in to anchor, so there was little loss of human life. However, like many others, the majority of the Third Field Kenpei had to abandon ship for the open sea. Sergeant[8] Akabori and several men under him were killed in the battle.

[1026] The Kenpeitai command and the Fourth Company landed near Frawan [?] Promontory in Banten Bay, where we cremated Sergeant Major Akabori and his men killed in battle, and set out to capture any remnant enemy troops and collect secret documents escaping from the destroyed vessels.

Closely following the army's take-over of Batavia on March 3, the Kenpeitai command and the Fourth Company set out for Batavia via Serang on March 5. Closing in on Serang, we discovered that the retreating Dutch Indies army had felled trees on both sides of the road between Serang and Batavia to block our advancing Japanese forces. As soon as the Kenpeitai command and Taniguchi's company marched into Batavia, we immediately took over the law school to the south of Gambir plaza in the center of the city. Here we established our Kenpeitai headquarters and the headquarters of the Fourth Company, and set to work.[9]

We Kenpei began immediately to direct the local police, round up remnant enemy soldiers, and manage the military supplies. We secured vital natural resources, put a check on looting by the natives, generally maintained civil order, and interned important persons. In particular, we interned in Struiswijk prison in Batavia some four hundred enemy Dutch, Australians, English and Americans, which excluded only a few

---

7 For a description of the Battle of Banten Bay, see F. C. Van Oosten, *The Battle of Java Sea* (Annapolis: Naval Institute Press, 1976), pp. 55-60.
8 The rank designated in the original Japanese is *sōchō*. *Sōchō* overlaps the following two ranks in the United States army: Sergeant Major of the Army, and Command Sergeant Major. In cases such as this where a Japanese rank overlaps two or more American ranks, we have used the highest rank equivalent in the United States army system. Koh Masuda, ed., *Kenkyusha's New Japanese-English Dictionary* (Tokyo: Kenkyusha, 1974), pp. 2102-3.
9 The Kenpeitai headquarters later moved to the Institute of Technology (*Gaishi*, p. 1110).

priests and innocuous half-breeds.[10]

The Japanese landing on Java was complete by March 4. The main force of the army had already departed on the Bandung offensive, when we discovered that the remaining Dutch Indies troops were hiding out in the mountains along the Serang River. The Satō platoon, a military command reserve squad, was immediately dispatched on a subjugation mission. It set out for its destination some 800 meters high up in the mountains, accompanied by Kenpeitai Warrant Officer Moriki and three of his Kenpei. The offensive resulted in the surrender of one Dutch Indies company and a police chief and his wife, as well as the capture of some twenty US and Australian soldiers who had been roaming about in the area. By the end of March the detachment had finished its mopping up operations in the area and returned to the home unit.

Meanwhile the Thirds Company commanded by Captain Sugō Shūzō had been on the *Ryūjōmaru*, the same ship Commander Imamura was on, at the time of the landing. The ship was heavily damaged under enemy attack, and ran aground. The entire crew had jumped ship into the oil-covered sea, but rescued with death at their shoulders the military command who had taken cover in their cabins.

After landing, the Third Company joined the main force of the Second Division (commanded by Lieutenant General Maruyama Masao) in subsequent attacks on Rawairian [Leuwiliang] and Buitenzorg [Bogor].[11] On the afternoon of March 9, we followed the front line units

---

[10] The Japanese word *konketsu* translates literally as "mixed blood," and refers here to Eurasians. Konketsu is a derogatory term in Japanese, hence the translation "half-breed" used here. Many prewar Japanese valued racial purity highly and thought of children of interracial unions as being somehow inferior. Prior to the twentieth century, a child of mixed race was usually called an *ai no ko*, which means both "in-between child" and "lovechild." The term *ai no ko* was originally used to refer to youthful Kabuki actors who were neither children nor fully adult. The term clearly had negative connotations however; it was also used to refer to mongrel dogs, for instance.

During World War II the term konketsu first came into frequent usage as a means to refer to GI babies and children of Japanese servicemen abroad. In defining the term konketsu the *Nihon Kokugo Daijiten* cites the following from the Yokomitsu Riichi novel *Shangai*: "If you do that, all you will be left with is a half-breed problem." Nihon Daijiten Kankōkai, ed., *Nihon Kokugo Daijiten* (Tokyo: Sho-gakkan, 1972-76), 8:484. The negative connotations of the term are apparent from the tone employed here. Nowadays the word konketsu is rarely used; the preferred term for children of mixed race is *hafu*, from the English term "half."

[11] The Second Division of the army spearheaded the invasion on West Java, while the Forty-eighth Division coming from the Philippines invaded Bali and East Java. Van Oosten, *Battle of the Java Sea*, pp. 77-78.

as they triumphantly entered Bandung city and then we Kenpei began operations.

The Second Company, commanded by Captain Kobayashi Shōkichi, became the Kenpeitai officially attached to the Forty-eighth Division of the army (commanded by Lieutenant General Tsuchihashi Isao). On February 19 the Forty-eighth Division set sail from Jolo[12] Island for its landing site on Java: Flangan [?Brondong] in the Surabaya province. As the division approached Flangan the troopships were heavily bombed by the United States air force, and the units were forced to scatter upon landing.

[1027] Everywhere the Japanese troops landed law and order were disrupted. The natives took advantage of the opportunity violently to ransack the homes of the Chinese and the whites. They ran off with all items of any value, as though they were avenging hundreds of years of resentment in one terrifying sweep. Seeing this graphic illustration of the natives' deep-rooted hostility, Kenpei Captain Kobayashi realized how extremely harsh the colonial policies of the Dutch governor general must have been. But now that the Japanese army had moved in, the violence of the natives was to be left unchecked no longer. Captain Kobayashi ordered his men to make every effort to restore civil order immediately.

The strength of the Kobayashi company and the Forty-eighth Division crushed the enemy *Taypu Kerutosono Jonpan*, and successfully penetrated and occupied Surabaya on March 8. One section of Kobayashi's company was assigned to the "Sumatran operations"[13] in central Java, where it was in charge of enforcing law and order in the Semarang district. Once order had been restored, the section returned to the Kobayashi company headquarters.

The First Kenpeitai Company under Captain Yajima Shichisaburō was attached to the Thirty-eighth Division (commanded by Lieutenant General Sano Tadayoshi), and had separated from the main Kenpeitai force at Cam Ranh Bay in the first half of February. To capture the Dutch territory of southern Sumatra, the Thirty-eighth Division moved upstream along the Musi River on February 15, landing in Palembang on February

---

12 Horo in *rōmaji*.
13 Sumatoran in *rōmaji*. One Japanese scholar speculates that "Sumatran Operations" may have been a special term used by the Japanese to indicate a particular kind of military strategy.

18. When the division arrived, Palembang was already occupied by the Japanese army, our paratroopers having landed on February 14.[14]

On March 12 the Imperial Guard Division of the Twenty-fifth Army landed in northern Sumatra to undertake the victorious central and northern Sumatran operations; the battle proceeded smoothly because the Dutch Indies forces had already unconditionally surrendered as of March 9.[15] The army took over Medan, the capital of Sumatra, and Padang on the central western coast, and by March 17 the central and northern mopping-up operations were complete.

During the closing days of the operations a provisional Kenpei detachment comprised of sixty men led by Lieutenant Colonel Yokota Masataka arrived. The detachment had formerly been with the Kenpeitai attached to the Twenty-fifth Army (commanded by Lieutenant Colonel Ōishi Masayuki). Second Lieutenant Ueno's Kenpeitai unit[16] was also dispatched to Palembang, where it relieved the Yajima company. Ever since landing a month and a half before, the Yajima company had been hard at work sweeping up remnant enemy troops, securing vital natural resources, and generally upholding civil order. At the time the Sumatran residents in the Palembang area were cooperating with the Japanese army, and conditions were almost too peaceful for the Kenpeitai. Now that it was being replaced, the Yajima company set sail from Palembang Bay on April 5 and returned to the Third Field Kenpeitai command in Batavia on April 8.

The Java Kenpeitai

Mopping-up operations on Java wound up in March 1942. The Third Field Kenpeitai deployed its men to maintain law and order in crucial areas throughout Java. After the take-over, Lieutenant General Imamura Hitoshi, Commander of the Sixteenth Army, [1028] ordered us to put

---

14 The purpose of this digression on Sumatra is to provide background on the Yajima company, which subsequently moved to Java.
15 "Within ten days in March of 1942 the approximately 55,000 men in the Sixteenth Army who had landed before the enemy had forced some 80,000 Dutch soldiers to surrender" (*Gaishi*, p. 1111).
16 A Kenpeitai unit (*buntai*) was a section of the Kenpeitai corps of indeterminate size, usually ranging between fifteen and thirty men. A unit dispatched smaller *bunkentai*, or detachments, for special missions.

all Dutch, starting with the governor general and his wife, government personnel, and the directors of powerful government-related companies into detention camps within Batavia city. Soldiers and military personnel were put into prisoner-of-war camps and prisons respectively. Separate detention camps just for women were set up, where boys and girls under the age of sixteen were also interned.[17]

Java was a complicated mix of races. Besides the Dutch, there were many Dutch-Indonesian half-breeds, as well as overseas Chinese, Ambonese, Indonesians, and Menadonese. In the government and various governmental organizations, the positions were invariably held by the Dutch and by the half-breeds, who were appointed as minor officials. The half-breeds and the overseas Chinese had the economic power, while the native Indonesians, Ambonese, and Menadonese were extremely poor.

After proclaiming a military government, the Sixteenth Army appointed particularly those half-breeds who had pledged cooperation with the military to positions in the central military administration, public corporations, and general manufacturing industries. The half-breeds continued to be entrusted with virtually all military administration, just as they had been under the former governor general. They were also appointed to posts in the central military administration.[18]

The Sixteenth Army command, the military administration command, and the Kenpeitai headquarters were all established in the Dutch Indies capital of Batavia.

At the end of April 1942 the Third Field Kenpeitai was renamed the Sixteenth Army Kenpeitai (commonly called the Java Kenpeitai) and was reorganized as follows:

---

[17] "The detention centers housing Dutch army prisoners were extremely open prisons without wire fencing," write the ex-Kenpei in *Gaishi*. "They didn't try to escape because they feared being attacked by the Indonesian people." (*Gaishi*, p. 1122.) An American civilian internee quotes the Japanese commandant of her internment camp as announcing on the first night "You Americans are merciful, but we Japanese do not know mercy. If anyone attempts to escape, he will be killed. If anyone does escape we will choose ten of you at random, and you will be shot . . . " The killing of other inmates upon the escape of one was a common policy, and an effective deterrent to escape attempts. Judy Hyland, *In the Land of the Rising Sun* (Minneapolis: Ausburg Publishing House, 1984), p. 24.

[18] The repetition of this fact belies the Kenpeitai's incredulity that Eurasians would be trusted with such a vital task.

The Sixteenth Army Kenpeitai

July 1941—Third Field Kenpeitai established
April 1942—Became Sixteenth Army Kenpeitai
Headquarters—Batavia
Commandant—Lieutenant Colonel Kuzumi Kenzaburō
Vice Commander—Captain Takayabu Saichirō
Chief of the Tokkō—Major Ikeyama Yasushi
Total force: 30 officers
Warrant officers and noncommissioned officers: 492
Total: 522
Batavia unit (Tanjung Priok detachment) Commander—Major Taniguchi Kiyoshi
Serang unit Commander—Second Lieutenant Onishi Kyūtarō
Bogor unit (Sukabumi detachment) Commander—Second Lieutenant Taniguchi Takeji
Bandung unit (Tasikamalaya detachment) Commander—Captain Sugō Shūzo
Cirebon unit (Tegal detachment) Commander—Captain Matsuoka Takezō
Solo unit (Madelang [?][19] detachment)
Purwokerto unit (Cilacap detachment) Commander—First Lieutenant Katō Michitarō
Yogyakarta unit (Magelang detachment) Commander—First Lieutenant Satō Heikichi
Semarang unit (Pekalongan detachment) Commander—Captain Yajima Shichisaburō
Surabaya unit (Wharf detachment; Bojonegoro detachment) Commander—Captain Kobayashi Shōkichi[20]
Malang unit (Kediri detachment; Probolinggo detachment) Commander—First Lieutenant Inoyama Jirō
Jember unit (Banyuwangi detachment) Commander—Captain Wada Kunishige

---

19 Maderan in *rōmaji*.
20 *Gaishi* notes that this is an error: Major Yanase Kasuku, and not Kobayashi, was the commander of the Surabaya unit. (*Gaishi*, p. 1109).

Surakarta unit (Madiun detachment; Yogya detachment)
Commander—First Lieutenant Ōnishi Katsuhiko

[1029] After we Japanese had proclaimed our military government, the Indonesians were the warmest to us, as was their nature, followed by the Ambonese and Menadonese. With the exception of one circle, the overseas Chinese were also relatively pro-Japanese.[21] There were a great many Chinese, and they were financially far better off than the Malaysians. The problem was the Dutch-Indonesian half-breeds who superficially cooperated but were actually extremely anti-Japanese. From the very beginning they were the cancer afflicting the body politic. The other very troublesome factor for the Kenpeitai in Java was the infiltration of spies from nearby Australia.

The climate in Java is similar to that in Japan just before the rainy season begins about the end of May. In the afternoon there is often a brief squall and the heat abates for a while. The rainy season begins at the end of August and lasts for about two months, although it rarely rains all day long even during this season. For clothing a short-sleeved shirt will do during the day and you only need one blanket for sleeping at night. The temperature varies a good deal in Indonesia even though it is in the tropics, because of the mountain ranges. The temperature drops five degrees if you climb a 300-meter hill. The Dutch and Chinese country cottages are located on the outskirts of town in the hills, where it is a different world indeed.

The tallest mountain on Java is Mt. Semeru, which towers 3,676 meters. Being a volcanic region, Java has many hot springs. There are no very large rivers but several well-known ones including the Solo, Brantas, and the Citarum.[22] Kenpeitai Captain Iizuka Kinjirō[23] remembers the island of Java as having a most suitable climate for the Japanese, and being a rather fine place to live. The ground is fertile and every last bit is cultivated to

---

21 Pro-Indonesian and pro-Chinese sympathies resound more clearly in the *Gaishi*. "Looking back on the history of the Kenpeitai and their relations with the natives in occupied territories, relations with the Indonesians and the overseas Chinese were especially good," write the authors, "... The warmth of the Indonesians is racially determined, and explains the dearth of violence committed towards women by the [Japanese] military and personnel." (*Gaishi*, pp. 1111-12).
22 Chitarumu in *rōmaji*.
23 Iizuka Kinjirō is the Zenkenren editor of this chapter on Java in the *Seishi*.

grow such major products as rice and corn, and oil is produced on a small scale. According to a military survey, the population at the time was 20 million.[24]

No sooner had the Kenpeitai taken on the responsibility of maintaining civil order and conducting counterespionage activities, than the number of anti-Japanese incidents began to grow. Let us now turn to an explanation of the sort of incidents with which each Kenpeitai unit had to grapple.

An Incident Under the Direct Control of Kenpeitai Headquarters

In July of 1942, enemy aircraft and submarines began attacking Japanese vessels transporting arms, ammunition, and other military supplies from Java to New Guinea and the Ambon islands. Our ships were being sunk one after the other, particularly in the Flores and Banda Seas. The damage just kept on increasing. The Japanese military command suspected enemy involvement even prior to the ships' departures, and ordered a close investigation by the Kenpeitai. We Kenpei judged that the spies based on Java were relaying information about the departing ships to the enemy, and that this could only be done by radio. In December of 1943 more than ten men in the Central China Kenpeitai Radio-Probe Squad, led by Second Lieutenant Muratomi Yoshio, were dispatched to Java to work with our Java Kenpeitai.

[1030] The critical investigation had been under way for some time, but the spies still remained on the loose. The military command and the Kenpeitai decided to strengthen the radio-probe squads by sending some thirty superior military communications unit members and ten or so noncommissioned Kenpei to a radio training school in Kuala Lumpur on the Malay peninsula. Over a three-month period military radio communications unit chief First Lieutenant Yoshie Yasuyuki and Kenpeitai Warrant Officer Yamazaki Toshio trained some eighty special radio-probe squad members. Thus, through our combined efforts, the military communications unit and the Kenpeitai spawned one large intelligence network.

---

24 This figure is a gross underestimate. In 1945 the population of Java was over 41 million. (Kanahele, "Japanese Occupation of Indonesia," p. 65.)

In May of 1944 the special radio-probe squads began working with various Kenpeitai units throughout the island of Java in an effort to identify suspicious radio signals. Nonetheless we were somehow unable to capture these spy culprits before the end of the war, although we were positive of their existence. After Japan met defeat, Yoshie's special radio-probe squads played an active role in the Indonesian independence movement at the time of Sukarno's kidnapping.[25] All the squad members were eventually arrested as suspected war criminals, while most of the enlisted men who were not Kenpei returned to their units scotfree.[26]

Rebellion, Intelligence, and Espionage

Japan had plunged into the Greater East Asia War in December 1941, and by March 9, 1942 our army had invaded Java and forced the Dutch army to surrender. In the interim the Dutch had roughly three months time to prepare for the Japanese occupation. By the time our Japanese army made its advance, the Dutch authorities had already established a powerful intelligence network using armed radio spies which spanned all of Indonesia. They tended to use the pro-Dutch half-breeds, the Menadonese, and the Ambonese, sending the inexperienced ones to Australia early on to be trained in espionage. One can see from this experience just how ingeniously the Dutch colonialists had operated for the past three hundred and fifty years. No wonder the half-breeds tried to highlight their Dutch white man's blood! And they used it well—to be appointed to positions in the military and government, where they served as an important base for the intelligence network.

Indeed the half-breeds had secured a decent livelihood and social standing for themselves under the Dutch. But it was doubtful that the status quo would be maintained under the Japanese occupation since, in spite of appearing to cooperate with us, in their hearts the half-breeds [1031] were secretly praying for the return of Dutch rule. You can see here the difficulty of colonial rule faced by the Japanese military administration which had to use them, because they knew everything, to maintain the

---

25 We learn later that the Kenpeitai failed to recover the kidnapped Sukarno, even with the assistance of the radio-probe squads. (*Gaishi*, p. 1221).
26 Another demonstration, to the Kenpei, of the injustice of the war crime trials.

civilian administration. Clearly, the creation of the half-breeds, like the making of intellectual poverty among the natives, was a link in the shrewd Dutch policy. For us Kenpei, who sought only to maintain peace and protect the army, this continual spying under a military government was bound to turn the half-breeds into our bitterest of enemies. Naturally when the war ended in Japan's defeat we Kenpei found ourselves up against the recriminations of the half-breeds and others on the Dutch side.

However, the Japanese army was narrowly saved by the existence of the native Indonesians. They were not especially anti-Japanese and, although they even rioted with a fiery surge of independence at the time of the Japanese defeat, they were essentially of a gentle nature. Since they were extremely poorly off, being socially controlled by the Dutch and the half-breeds, and economically suppressed by the half-breeds and the overseas Chinese, they partook in almost no anti-Japanese activity. In fact, the remarkable thing about Java and Sumatra was that the Dutch government had taken great pains to ensure that there were very few problems with Communist activity.[27]

When the Sixteenth Army occupied Java, we put Governor General van Mook and the chief officials in his government, the Dutch Indies Commander Lieutenant General Ter Poorten, some 93,000 Dutch Indies troops, and approximately 5,000 American, British, and Australian troops and military personnel into prisoner-of-war camps in the Batavia area.[28] Mrs. van Mook and other civilian personnel who had Dutch citizenship were placed in a separate detention camp. How we Kenpei struggled to maintain law and order and combat the local spying activity! An account of the sorts of incidents encountered by our various units follows.

Around June of 1942 in Batavia, just as the Sixteenth Army military administration was getting underway, a rumor that "the Japanese will soon lose the war, and the Dutch forces will return, so that those who have been cooperating with the Japanese will be punished as traitors" began circulating from God knows where. In order to gauge the effect of this rumor on public opinion, the Batavia Kenpeitai undertook an

---

27 Suppression of communists was a primary function of the Kenpeitai in Japan.
28 This information is clearly erroneous, as Lieutenant-Governor H. J. van Mook escaped to Australia on March 7, 1942, the day before the Allied forces were surrendered to the Japanese. See Walter B. Maass, *The Netherlands at War: 1940-45* (London: Abelard-Schuman, 1970), p. 100.

investigation and discovered that the rumor had originated in the detention center for Dutch women and children. Batavia unit commander Major Taniguchi Kiyoshi then launched a careful investigation within the detention center on the off chance that the principal offender was one of the women detainees. The culprit turned out to be none other than the Governor General van Mook's wife, who had had permission to travel to and from the camp and had been secretly listening to foreign radio broadcasts. Knowing the propaganda reports of the British and American side, she was deliberately spreading this rumor. Major Taniguchi immediately confiscated the radio but [1032] simply scolded and warned the governor general's wife.[29]

In September our Batavia Kenpeitai unit detected that some half-breed gas company employees were plotting to help the Allied forces land. We Kenpeitai also knew well that the half-breeds were anti-Japanese. However, severely punishing all the half-breed employees would clearly have necessitated the suspension of all gas company activity. We therefore chose to arrest only ten half-breeds and give them light sentences.[30]

In another incident, on a Japanese holiday when the Sun flag was raised, the [Japanese] anthem was sung, and "Banzai" was to come at the end, half-breed employees refused to cry "Banzai," saying "We are not Japanese." This came to be known as the "Anti-Japanese Banzai Refusal Incident."

This sort of incident abounded. Around February 1943 the wife of a Dutch businessman named N [?] in Batavia was arrested for disseminating a rumor similar to that spread by the Dutch governor general's wife. Another incident involved a public corporation managed by the Dutch that handled tobacco, coffee, sugar, and palm oil, and employed some 1,000 half-breeds. The Batavia Kenpeitai unit discovered that these half-breeds, who had continued to be employed even after military rule had been established, were storing up weapons, and forming an underground organization in preparation for an uprising on the occasion of an Allied

---

29 Had the offending person carried less rank, she might have been treated a great deal less leniently. For a first-hand account of the tortures suffered by one Australian prisoner-of-war who was caught assembling a short-wave radio, see Russell, *Knights of Bushido,* pp. 194-98.
30 This incident demonstrates how much the Japanese army relied on local personnel and resources to conduct its war.

landing. All involved were arrested in April 1943, and dozens of the main criminals were sent to the Kenpeitai headquarters, after we had gathered such undeniable evidence as weapons and other espionage material.

At headquarters the incident was immediately assigned to the Tokkō division.[31] But, in the midst of investigating this incident, the Kenpeitai headquarters became so overwhelmed by time constraints, the frequency of incidents, and a shortage of hands that we ended up being unable to afford the time to conduct martial law proceedings scrupulously.[32] Major Murase Mitsuo, chief of the Tokkō division at the time, therefore received approval from Lieutenant General Harada Kumakichi[33] to sentence or take severe measures with those whose investigations had been concluded and for whom suspicion had been established, without holding martial law proceedings. "Severe measures" meant execution, or *"kikōsaku"* as we Kenpeitai called it.[34]

By this time—July 1943—the Japanese forces had already lost at Guadalcanal, and had met honorable defeat in the dead of winter on Attu

---

[31] *Tokkō* is an acronym for Tokubetsu Kōtō Keisatsu [Special Higher Police], commonly known as the thought control police. See Translators' Preface.

[32] A martial law proceeding *[gunritsu kaigi]* was a summary procedure used by the Japanese military in occupied territories to inflict punishment on wrongdoers from enemy armies or the local populace. As compared with a court martial *[gunpō kaigi]*, a martial law proceeding provided the accused with no right to present a defense. No law or edict expressly authorized the use of martial law proceedings, but the Kenpeitai argued that the right to use such proceedings was encompassed by the military commander-in-chief's "authority of supreme command." According to the *Seishi*, it was common practice for military judge advocates to receive directives on martial law proceedings from the military chiefs of staff, who had only to report their policies to the commander-in-chief. Ex-Kenpei claim that in a martial law proceeding "the substance of the trial was nowhere completely different from a court martial . . . [and] should be regarded with equal respect." *(Seishi*, p. 1246.) These summary proceedings were popularly called "Kenpeitai proceedings" among the Japanese because the judge advocates, prosecutors, and judges were often all Kenpei. An explanation and defense of gupritsu kaigi by a former Kenpei appears in Miyazaki Kiyotaka, *Gunpō Kaigi* [Courts Martial], (Tokyo: Fuji Shobō, 1953).

[33] Japanese Commander-in-Chief of the Sixteenth Army in Java, November 1942-April 1945.

[34] Dr. Tetsuya Kataoka coined the phrase "Operation Hades" as an appropriate translation for this Kenpeitai internal code word. *Kikōsaku* is a compound word, the first character of which comes from the Buddhist term *Kōsen* ["yellow spring"], which is an abode for the dead in Asian mythology. The underground spring was known as the "yellow spring" because yellow was the color of the earth in China, where the myth originated. While Kōsen was originally simply a land where all dead people go, as distinct from the Buddhist notion of hell, nowadays particularly in Japan the two notions (Hades and Hell) are confounded in most people's minds. Nihon Daijiten Kankōkai, ed., *Nihon Kokugo Daijiten* (Tokyo: Shogakkan, 1972-76), 7:532. It is fair to assume, then, that the word kōsen, and hence the prefix *ki*, had a hellish connotation to the Kenpeitai. The second two syllables of the term kikōsaku mean engineering, construction, manoeuvering and the like, and are best translated as "Operation."

Island; Navy Admiral Yamamoto Isoroku had been killed in battle; and day by day the tide of war was turning against the Japanese forces. Even on Java the anti-Japanese activity was mounting and the frequency of incidents was making the Kenpeitai nervous. It was at this point that the Chief of the Tokkō division, Major Murase, decided that following the normal procedure from the reporting of an incident through to the martial law court proceedings, was hindering us Kenpei from accomplishing our duties.[35] The army was being paralyzed, and the work of the military government being impeded.[36]

[1033] The word kikōsaku comes from the word *Kōsen*.[37] Even though the Kenpeitai had been under murderous pressure[38] at the time, the Dutch side viewed the omission of martial law proceedings as an illegal act, and after the war it was used as a pretext for accusing the Kenpeitai of war crimes. But the Kenpei who were there at the time remember that both the Kenpei and the private first-class soldiers were well aware that kikōsaku was illegal. But they claim that realistically, since not a single day had passed quietly without having to cope with countless incidents, honorably conducting martial law proceedings would have completely paralyzed both the Kenpeitai and military headquarters. They also claim that the normal citizens were at fault, for they knew that it was a crime for them, to say nothing of a soldier, to be forming schemes for spying or rebelling in any way against an occupying army during wartime.

In any event, the decision to perform kikōsaku involved the investigation by each unit of the incident, and the reporting of the incident to headquarters. If the army commander gave his approval, it was permissible for the unit to execute the criminal on the spot. This sort of execution was called kikōsaku.[39]

---

35 The Dutch executed Murase by firing squad in Glodok prison on November 3, 1949. After being sentenced to death, Murase wrote to his subordinates awaiting their executions in the same cell block of his non-attachment to life: "now, for my life, I have not even the slightest lingering affection; nor for my death, have I the slightest remorse ..." See *Isho*, pp. 443-45.
36 The *Gaishi* authors cite the July 1943 series of kikōsaku as one of the three main events that took place during wartime in Java, in the minds of ex-Kenpei. The other two major incidents were the Tasikmalaya Revolt and the Blitar Rebellion (see forthcoming discussion in text). *[Gaishi*, p. 1112.)
37 See footnote 34 above.
38 It is unclear whether this pun was intentional, but surely the irony of the choice of adjective is evident in retrospect.
39 In the Tokyo War Crimes Trial a Major Katsumura, former operations officer of the Java Kenpeitai

But one anti-Japanese conspiracy incident involving the Saibai Corporation led to a fairly serious error on the part of the Batavia Kenpeitai unit. The investigation into this incident was carried out by the chief of the Tokkō division at the Kenpeitai headquarters. The arrests were made by the Batavia unit, to whom headquarters had sent a list of those to be executed in three months. Thirteen persons were executed in connection with this incident. Among the names on the roster was the newly identified ringleader of the conspiracy, whom the Batavia unit set off to arrest immediately. The subject was at the home of a Dutch clergyman. When the Kenpei arrived, a young woman about twenty-four years old came out of the house and, declaring that she was the person on the roster, gave herself up for arrest. The true criminal was really this woman's younger brother, but the young woman protected her brother knowing that she would be killed. The Kenpei failed to detect the truth,

---

headquarters in Batavia gave evidence admitting to execution without trial in the so-called "ki" case in which, according to the prosecution's summary of Katsumura's report, "239 persons were executed in strict secrecy.... In order to settle the case as soon as possible, this case was dealt with on the spot. The investigation officer decided whether to inflict the death sentence and his decision was approved by the higher officials on the authority of the commander-in-chief after examination by the staff officer for Kempei [sic] affairs at army headquarters." Major Katsu-mura also gave evidence about a similar "Ji" operation that took place in Sumatra in 1943. According to the prosecution's oral summary submitted as evidence of Katsumura's written report, the same system was used as in the "Ki" operation in Java: "The suspects were not sent up to Court Martial but a speedy way of dealing with them was adopted. . . . When the crime was clearly proved—in the opinion of the torturing investigators—and the death sentence was considered suitable, the criminals were executed, on the decision of the Army. These executions were carried out fortnightly by every detachment of every section, in secrecy. The executions were at once reported to Kempei [sic] headquarters, who at once reported to the Army." R. John Pritchard and Sonia M. Zaide, eds., *International Military Tribunal for the Far East: The Tokyo War Crimes Trial: The Proceedings,* 22 vols. (New York: Garland, 1981), 6: 13701-702, 13810. *International Military Tribunal for the Far East: The Tokyo War Crimes Trial: Index and Guide,* 5 vols. (New York: Garland, 1981-85), 3: 226, 228.

In "Self-criticism by the Kenpei," a three page section toward the end of the *Seishi*, the authors have the following to say about the executions they committed without a trial: "In the southern occupied territories, especially in the islands, there were many instances in which enemy air force pilots were executed without martial law proceedings *[gunritsu kaigi]*. Conditions were such that there were inevitably no judge advocates, and communication with [those conducting] martial law proceedings had been cut off, but all the same, in whatever case in the army, one should probably always offer the opinion to one's superior that trials should be enforced. Even if it was a military order, we cannot nod in approval at the fact that the Kenpei themselves, who had a responsibility to uphold the legal system, executed prisoners of war without a trial. Also, as far as the execution of prisoners of war is concerned, in the war crimes trials the Allied armies pointed out the atrocity of decapitation. Because it is clearly stated in martial law that death should be by shooting, the Kenpei should have followed this guideline in offering to their superiors their opinion on the method of execution." *(Seishi,* p. 1299.)

since the roster was in English and the family names of the woman and her brother were the same, and because it was not at all unusual for women to take part in these kind of activities.

The young woman kept quiet and covered up for her brother until the very end, when she was executed along with the twelve criminals. The Kenpei sympathized with and were deeply impressed by the woman's quiet composure, but when the orders came they could not help but obey.

When a letter of complaint was issued by the woman's family after the war, headquarters and the Batavia unit Kenpei were astonished. Until the letter of complaint came out, we had had no idea that the girl had been a substitute. It was probably inevitable that this mistake was treated as a war crime. This woman who kept silent, uttering not a word in her defense to the very end, was really admirable, and remains a heart-rendering memory in the minds of the Kenpei from those days.

[1034] In August 1943 we Kenpei uncovered an attempt at anti-Japanese conspiracy led by the Dutch professor Bijirusuma [?] and other school officials. About the same time we also detected an anti-Japanese plot led by three Indian-European half-breeds, who were clearly storing up weapons for an armed uprising. The culprits were executed via kikōsaku. Then, in mid-September, a group of several dozen Ambonese night watchmen in Surabaya was arrested wholesale for using fireworks during the daytime to guide the Australian air forces to bombing targets and important facilities.

In February 1944 the world-famous Indonesian microbiologist Dr. Maruzuki was arrested by the Batavia Kenpeitai. Unhappy that the natives were being rounded up to work at military facilities, Dr. Maruzuki caused an outbreak of dysentery among the workers by injecting dysentery bacteria into their normal preventive vaccines. Incapacitating the workers was a plot to obstruct Japanese military construction.

We Kenpei were suspicious of the sudden outbreak of dysentery among the laborers, and proceeded to conduct investigations. The investigations took over three months, if only because the laborers were naturally unsanitary; they became a sort of blind spot in our investigations, causing unforeseen delays. But eventually it was discovered that Professor Maruzuki's injections were to blame.

We Kenpei realized early on that Professor Maruzuki was a man of influence in pro-Dutch circles and popular among the Indonesians, so he was treated with extreme caution from the moment of his arrest through to the investigations. Accordingly, his punishment was relatively light.

In April, midway through the Maruzuki investigation, the public railway administrative offices throughout the island erupted in an attempt at rebellion. This incident may have been an outgrowth of the Saibai Corporation incident of May 1913, as the two organizations were related. The plot had been engineered by all the corporation officials on the entire island, including the very director of the Railway Corporation. Their aim was to destroy the railway network and aid the counteroffensive Allied landing. After a careful investigation was carried out jointly by the Batavia, Semarang, and Purwokerto Kenpeitai units, the top brass was arrested simultaneously in the three respective places and the principal offenders were executed by kikōsaku.

The Batavia unit was extremely busy, with incident after incident cropping up in a row. We Kenpei got burned, especially by false rumors invented by the mixed bloods and Chinese. The Robbs-Carlton [?][40] incident was just such a case in point, but a truly more serious incident occurred in the military command in 1945.

[1035] The military command had an international broadcast station which disseminated propaganda among the natives. Four Dutch-Indonesian half-breeds did the translation work. They often secretly listened to our military headquarters short wave radio, and after work would spread news that was not helpful to the Japanese army (such things as where the Japanese forces had been wiped out on such and such an island, where the Allied forces were landing on Java, that the Japanese were sure to lose, and so on). This sort of news began spreading around the middle of 1944, but even the Kenpeitai could not easily identify the source of these reports. The source was indeed within the military command: the beacon does not shine on its own base. By the time the

---

40 Robesu-Carudon in *rōmaji*.

Kenpeitai investigations revealed that the four half-breeds had indeed been responsible it was already June, and the war ended midway through the arrests and investigations. This was the last of the incidents like the incidents handled by the Batavia Kenpeitai.

Then there was the Bogor Kenpei Unit. Soon after it was formed, the Bogor Unit took over the job of handling the rumors circulated by the anti-Japanese Briatsu Society[41] conspiracy. In July, this unit encountered its most serious incident. The Dutch army surrendered as soon as the Japanese army occupied Java. A young Dutch First Lieutenant named Welter commanded one of the companies, and at the time of his surrender had pledged to cooperate with the Japanese and spy for our side. But the Kenpeitai discovered that Welter was actually organizing an espionage ring with the help of eighty half-breeds in Bogor behind our backs. First Lieutenant Welter was arrested, sent to martial law proceedings,[42] and finally executed.[43] But it turned out that Welter was the son of a former Dutch Prime Minister. After the war First Lieutenant Welter's death in Java was glorified in Holland as an heroic anti-Japanese act.

In a similar incident, the Dutch officer Captain Wernink capitulated, pledged assistance to the Japanese, and secretly began organizing an underground. He was also arrested and executed.[44]

Finally there were such failed attempts at espionage as the De Toortz [?] incident, the Pati conspiracy incident, and the Mulder [?] conspiracy, all ending in arrests.

The Bandung Kenpeitai, located some 130 kilometers to the southeast of Batavia, had to contend with the Kruisman[45] conspiracy, the plot by Dutch Captain deLange, and other incidents. deLange was executed during the war for being a spy.[46]

The important Japanese navy base was located in eastern Java in

---

41 Probably Briat, as in the Briat people of eastern Siberia. Usually spelled *Buriyatō* in Japanese.
42 *Gunritsu kaigi*.
43 First Lieutenant Welter was executed on May 15, 1943. Prof. Dr. I. J. Brugmans et al., eds., *Nederlandsch-Indie onder Japanse Bezetting: Gegevens en documenten over de jaren 1942-45* (Franeker: Uitgave T. Wever, 1960), p. 660.
44 Captain A.L.J. Wernink was executed in Batavia on December 12, 1944. Ibid., p. 660.
45 Kurisuman in *rōmaji*.
46 Captain R. G. deLange was accused of being the leader of an underground group in Bandung. He was executed by the Japanese in Batavia on April 10, 1943. Brugmans et al., eds., *Nederlandsch-Indie*, p. 645.

Surabaya across from Madura island. The Australian forces regarded the spot as a key strategic base because of its great ammunition, grain, and fuel storage capacity. It was also the target on Java [1036] most often bombarded by enemy air raids. The Surabaya unit was in charge of patrolling this area.

In August of 1943 the Surabaya unit detected an anti-Japanese plot fomenting, and immediately arrested several half-breeds working on a naval construction site. During the interrogations some Kenpei excessively tortured and killed one of the criminals. Consequently the Surabaya unit yielded eight war criminals after the defeat.

In September the unit arrested a spy ring operated largely by Ambonese. The group's aim had been to guide the Australian forces to bombing sites using flash signals.

In the latter part of 1943 Java began to be bombarded by the Australian forces. Surabaya was bombed repeatedly because of the naval base there. Ships leaving the bay were attacked by US submarines, which had learned the whereabouts of the vessels from spies. Some 65 kilometers south of Surabaya an oil-pipeline originally set up by the Dutch was destroyed a few times. The damage was relatively light and repairs did not require many days, but the Bojonegoro Kenpei lacked the manpower to patrol a pipeline of such length. Even while we kept strict guard, it was damaged again and again. Once we made the arrests, we found that half-breeds formed the nucleus of the sabotage ring in this case as well. As for the conspiracy to blow up the oil field, we made certain to arrest the spy rings before they made their attempts.

Incidents involving the Purwokerto Kenpeitai unit included the failed revolt of the public railway corporation mentioned earlier, which was the largest incident [encountered by this particular unit], an incident in which the Batavia and Semarang units were also involved, and the Overseas Chinese Linquan incident involving spies planted by the Dutch. The Kenpeitai detachment sent to Cilacap, an important port—the largest on the southern coast of Java—was busy keeping track of, investigating, and arresting armed spies dispatched at night by US and Australian submarines. A number of arrests were also made of half-bloods communicating with enemy submarines from remote areas on land. In other cases, people making their lives by the sea were arrested for communicating with English submarines navigating the Indian Ocean.

The Kediri unit on eastern Java to the southwest of Surabaya encountered the conspiracy of the people's Sarekat Islam party, a public pro-Dutch political society.[47] There were four incidents of arrests of armed infiltrators and about a dozen arrests of spies planted by the Dutch. In truth, there must have been a few times more than the arrested numbers.

[1037] At the time Java was already fairly developed and there were few areas that remained unexplored by man. The jungles were not very dense, so it was not easy for spies to hide. Although planted spies achieved some measure of success, infiltrating spies were easily detected. As Japan continued her offensive, the number of arrests continued to increase, but a number of Dutch officers escaped to Australia and returned to Java bringing with them several spies newly trained in Australia. The Kenpeitai occasionally patrolled the southern coast of Java because there were only a few coastlines where it was possible to land, but it was still easy for groups of armed spies that prepared carefully to infiltrate.

But then, the majority of spies used by the Kenpeitai were Dutch-Indonesian half-breeds. They misled the Kenpei who assessed information by intentionally spreading false rumors. In particular, there were more than a few occasions when we mistakenly made arrests, having been led on by false information.

The Tasikmalaya Revolt

Tasikmalaya, located in western Java between Bandung and Cilacap, was a large Muslim gathering place. Soon after the Japanese took over, the Muslim leader Mustafa began stirring up anti-Japanese sentiment, and clearly harboring plans to build an Islamic kingdom at the first opportunity. He was supported by approximately 3,000 devotees and adherents, so his influence could not be taken lightly. Do what it might, the Tasikmalaya Kenpeitai detachment was small and could not treat any

---

47 Sarikatto-aya in *rōmaji*. This was, of course, the oldest anti-Dutch nationalist party in Indonesia.

action lightly.

In March 1944 Mustafa incited an anti-Japanese riot. The local detachment sent Sergeants Kobayashi and Nakamikawa, Corporals Okuno and Kuwada, and local interpreters to the site to quell the riot and gather intelligence. In the midst of reconnoitering, Sergeants Kobayashi and Nakamikawa were sighted by the mob and slaughtered. Corporals Okuno and Kuwada barely escaped disaster and survived to report the situation to the local detachment.[48]

At this point the Tasikmalaya Kenpeitai unit commander became determined to crush the riot. He enlisted the support of one company of locally stationed infantry, mobilized over ten tank trucks, surrounded the rioters assembled at the church,[49] and ordered the mob to surrender. He was met with resistance; a battle ensued, but the riot was eventually crushed, with a death toll of several hundred. Mustafa and twenty-three under him were sent to their deaths following martial law proceedings,[50] while others were imprisoned in the government military detention unit. This was the greatest purely civilian rebellion in the history of the military government in Java, and clearly brought home to us the fearsome nature of religious rebellion.

The incident recalled the famous *"Ikkō ikki"*[51] of the Honganji sect

---

[48] General Yamamoto Motoshige, chief of the Japanese military administration, tells the story differently. According to Yamamoto, the Kenpei had come upon a gathering of Mustafa's students who were outfitted with spears in order to defend themselves against gangs of thieves terrorizing the neighborhood at the time. The Kenpei mistakenly believed the Muslims were organizing an anti-Japanese riot, approached Mustafa, and began to interrogate him using physical force. This incensed some people in the crowd, and led to the spontaneous outburst of violence. Kanahele, "Japanese Occupation of Indonesia," pp. 139-40. For other accounts of the Tasikmalaya revolt, see Benedict R. O'G. Anderson, *Java in a Time of Revolution: Occupation and Resistance, 1947-1946* (Ithaca: Cornell University Press, 1972), p. 35, and Harry J. Benda, *The Crescent and the Rising Sun* (The Hague, van Hoeve, 1958), pp. 159-61, 269, n. 48.

[49] Here the authors use the term *kyōkai*, which usually refers to a church, when they are really speaking of a mosque *(kaikyōjiin* in Japanese).

[50] Gunritsu kaigi.

[51] *Ikkō ikki* ["single-minded uprisings"] refers to uprisings led by a militant Buddhist sect called *Jōdo shinshū* [True Pure Land], which earned the epithet *ikkō* ["single-minded"] for its zealotry. The headquarters of the sect were in Honganji, the Temples of the Original Vow, in Kyoto. Perhaps partially because of its disregard for high ritual and emphasis on salvation through faith alone, the True Pure Land sect had a greater following among peasants than rival Buddhist sects that drew on support from samurai and noblemen. In the fifteenth and sixteenth centuries, the armed adherents of the True Pure Land sect clashed openly with their Buddhist rivals and the feudal warlords. They fought fiercely for ninety years, until they finally succumbed to the feudal landlords in 1580. (John K. Fairbank et al., *East Asia: Tradition and Transformation* [Cambridge: Harvard

in Japanese history, the uprisings that continued from the middle of the Muromachi period through to the time of the Warring States. The great sense of mission felt by the Ikkō ikki religious adherents who blindly followed their leaders confronted others with a very particular view of life and death, [1038] a religious conviction which feared not even death as a means to accomplish a goal. During the Tasikmalaya riot, when their leader gave his orders, the mob of believers, armed only with hatchets, charged for all they were worth at the surrounding Kenpei who called for their surrender, climbing over their dead comrades even as they fell under the fire of the Japanese forces. The ghastly sight of the mob closing in, with their hatchets above their heads, is said to have set even the Kenpei, with our vast battlefield experience, trembling in spite of ourselves.

There were considerable regional differences in degrees of faith among the Javanese Muslims, but at the time Tasikmalaya was an active area. The Islamic doctrine of afterlife *(Akhirat[52])* teaches that people are revived after death. Except that the idea that the good are blessed in heaven while the bad receive torture and suffering in hell is assuredly Buddhist. Also basic to Islam is the fatalistic tenet concerning God's will (Qadā) founded in an absolute belief in the one and only God Allah, and the belief that everything happens just as Allah wishes. Whenever the respected leader spouted his prophecies, the ignorant followers blindly believed. Because this incident took place on what was clearly Islamic ground, the Kenpeitai had a hard time dealing with it afterwards.[53]

When it comes to blind faith, communism shares something with religion. All along the Kenpeitai was involved in fateful show-downs with the Communist Party, but there was virtually no organized Communist Party in Java at the time.

University Press, 1978], p. 381. John W. Hall and Takeshi Toyoda, eds., *Japan in the Muromachi Age* [Berkeley: University of California Press, 1977] p. 123.)

52 *Aahira* in *rōmaji*.

53 In Sumatra as well, there were spontaneous outbursts against the Japanese. One incident, known to the Kenpeitai as the Raid of the Kotaraja Muslims, was triggered by a display of disrespect for Islamic culture by some Japanese soldiers. "Half as a joke, they [the Japanese soldiers] ate the carp that the natives were keeping in a bathing pool close to the church. Full of hatred for what the company had done to their sacred church, a mob of over 1,000 native Muslims attacked the company headquarters and slaughtered about forty Japanese soldiers. One Kenpei attached to the company was also killed. . . . From then on we Kenpei made a point of chatting with the Muslim leaders, and repaying the church which respected the ardent beliefs of the natives. In general, we strove to accustom ourselves to the Muslim way of life." (*Gaishi*, pp. 1132-33.)

The Indonesian Communist Party was formed in May 1920 (Taishō 9) as the first such party in Asia. At the time there was a considerable popular movement and the party received support from all social classes, but by 1927 western Sumatra and Java were undergoing full-scale revolution, and the Dutch authorities began to suppress the uprisings. Later, in 1945 when the Greater East Asia War ended, interest resurfaced with the Indonesian independence. Thus Java was the one place where there was virtually no Communist party.

The Rebellion of the Indonesian Volunteer Army[54]

In the latter half of 1943 the Japanese army established and began training the Indonesian volunteer army. Finally a sense of independence was beginning to awaken in the Indonesians. However in February 1945 Suprijadi, the commander of the volunteer army unit in Blitar in eastern Java, who was opposed to the rigorous Japanese army training and the wild private lifestyles of the Japanese officers, conspired with a dozen or more top cadres in the volunteer army. They called an emergency gathering of the entire battalion of 300 men, and all of the men deserted in full force. Had this been the only incident, it might have been easier to accept, but the regiment proceeded to attack the telephone bureau and the hotel where the Japanese officers were lodged, managing to kill both the telephone bureau director and the two half-breed female employees of the hotel, while injuring several others. This required the mobilization of the Kediri Kenpeitai detachment. With the help of the central and eastern defense corps, the Kediri Kenpeitai detachment [1039] began encouraging the deserting battalion to submit and quelled the rebellion. They arrested all of the men, with the exception of the ringleader Suprijadi,[55] and court-martialled ten cadres.[56]

---

54 In Japanese, the *giyūgun*. The authors of *Seishi* use the term giyūgun generally to refer to either of the two Japanese-trained Indonesian volunteer armies—(the Peta [Pembela Tanah Air—Volunteer Army of Defenders of the Fatherland] in Java and the giyūgun in Sumatra—or any of their units.
55 Suprijadi apparently vanished during the uprising, but no announcement of his death was ever made. He lived on as a legend and was appointed posthumously to the Indonesian cabinet as minister of the people's security in October 1945. (Anderson, *Java in a Time of Revolution*, pp. 11, n. 3; 232.)
56 The term used here is *gunpō kaigi ni sōchi-shita*, or court-martialled. No less than the full formality of a courts-martial could be expected, given the fact that the offenders were volunteer auxiliaries

In the Great East Asia War the most rebellion, conspiracy, and espionage occurred in Java and the Philippines. What was unique about Java was that so many stratagems were detected before completion. There was not a spot anywhere where there was a Kenpeitai unit or detachment that did not have any incidents. The Serang unit arrested four armed radio spies who had infiltrated via submarine, the Kediri unit seven armed spies commanded by a Dutch First Lieutenant, and a half-breed who made counterfeit coupons, for example. In another case the Kenpeitai, informed in advance by intelligence, apprehended armed spies landing by night in submarine-launched rubber boats. In this case the armed spies were arrested but not killed. The most important thing was not to let them operate their radios. Once spies have been in contact by radio, their arrest is of no value, because they cannot be used as double agents if they have already communicated their situation. Because they were armed spies, they were often equipped with portable light machine-guns. Consequently, there was a good possibility that those of us on the Kenpeitai side would be killed, and the arrest of armed spies was a life-risking operation.

Deplorable Incidents in the Army

In mid-1943 a Kenpeitai Company Commander (First Lieutenant) was murdered at the army veterinary hospital in Bandung. The Bandung Kenpeitai investigation was under way immediately and revealed that the culprit was a private[57] in his forties who had been an orderly for the victim. It was an unusual case in Java.

The private explained his motive to the Kenpeitai. The events had proceeded as follows according to the Kenpei record:[58] The private was aboard a ship transporting ailing horses when the ship was attacked and sunk by enemy aircraft. When the older private attempted to board a

---

trained by the Japanese themselves. Sukarno and other influential Indonesians were coerced into coming to the trial to make it look as though they condoned the disciplinary action being taken, but restraint was used in punishing the offenders to reduce the chance of a mass reprisal. (Ibid., p. 74, n. 32; Kanahele, "Japanese Occupation of Indonesia," p. 187.

57 The rank of *ittō-hei* in the Japanese army is equivalent to the rank of private E-2 in the United States army. Masuda Koh, ed., *Kenkyusha's New Japanese-English Dictionary*, pp. 2102-3.

58 *Kenpei Chōshō* in Japanese.

lifeboat with the rest of the soldiers, the company commander refused to allow him to get on, saying that there was not enough space for everyone and the eldest soldier should die first. The private was dangerously close to drowning when another lifeboat picked him up, but his hatred for the company commander never disappeared.

Later on the private became an orderly under the company commander. The young company commander lacked humanity and treated his soldiers pretty roughly. And so it was that the orderly ended up killing the company commander: the private took his own saber and stabbed the company commander to death. Of course the private also had his own emotional problems.

It being wartime, the killing of a superior was punishable by death. [1040] In the end the old enlisted man was court-martialled and executed, but the case gave much cause for thought.

One of the most difficult moral problems for the army at the time was the treatment of older conscripted men.[59] According to military regulations, young commissioned and noncommissioned officers and even veteran soldiers would have to train and command older new conscripts who had both social status and ability. It was utterly tragic when an older man was led by an inferior man. This was a structural problem with the army hierarchy that could not be helped, which necessarily led to much anxiety; it [the system] certainly would be unbearable were it not for humanitarian considerations. An excellent example of such a conflict can be seen in the case of Matsumae Shigeyoshi, the former Telecommunication Engineering Bureau Chief. At age forty-four, he was high-handedly conscripted as a second-class soldier for ruffling the feathers of Prime Minister Tōjō; the incident is a famous one in Shōwa history. Fortunately there were many in the military who sympathized with Matsumae and his levy was later cancelled.

There is no doubt that conscripting seniors as soldiers caused much grief in the army, where solidarity is a cardinal principle. Certainly an inexcusable lack of consideration for an older person played a part in the Bandung company commander murder case. Even today there must be

---

59 The Japanese army in Java had an unusually high proportion of older recruits, probably because Java was one of the least active combat zones among the occupied territories. Kanahele, "Japanese Occupation of Indonesia," pp. vi, 65.

many people who remember experiencing such treatment.[60]

There were also incidents of corruption within the army command. Over several years, as the initial occupation turned into a military administration, it was inevitable that military discipline became somewhat lax. Under tense wartime conditions, it is easy enough to uphold military discipline, but as the occupation moves away from the battlefield, men everywhere both east and west of the ocean lay bare their weaknesses.

We Java Kenpeitai were unique first in that we were at the mercy of the ingenious colonial policy of the Dutch. The Dutch-Indies colonial policy must be viewed as a success, at the very least. Their clever colonial policy was responsible for both the large number of Dutch-Indonesian half-breeds and the large number of pro-Dutch factions in other racial groups, as well as for the extensive intelligence network which the Dutch were putting the finishing touches on when the Japanese invaded. The intelligence activity was conducted by planted spies in cooperation with soldiers and residents who had supposedly surrendered, and developed into a full-scale anti-Japanese movement during the occupation. The onshore infiltration of armed spies from abroad also drew the entire island of Java into a vortex of stratagems.

For the sparsely equipped Kenpeitai, control and suppression[61] became a difficult task. Although it was easier geographically to control the investigations than it was in other areas, the sheer volume of incidents and arrests was a phenomenon unheard of in other Southern regions.

After the war ended in our defeat, [1041] the Java Kenpeitai turned out the greatest number of war criminals; this stemmed from Holland's

---

60 The story of Kitani recalls the harsh treatment suffered by the protagonist in *Zone of Emptiness*. For his failure to turn in the money in a wallet he found in a bathroom, which turned out to belong to a senior officer, the protagonist is imprisoned for two years, brutally treated by the Kenpei and his other superiors, and emotionally shattered. Hiroshi Noma, *Zone of Emptiness* (Cleveland: World Publishing, 1956), translated from Japanese to French by B. Frecht-man, and from French to English by H. de Boissel.
61 The two Japanese words *torishimari* ["control"] and *dan'atsu* ["suppression"] are combined here in the compound *torishimari-dan'atsu* which neatly summarizes the primary functions of the Kenpeitai. The noun torishimari comes from the verb *torishimaru*, meaning to control strictly, police, or manage. To explain the word, the *Nihon Kokugo Daijiten* cites the following from a short story by Natsume Sōseki: "The police pronounced that thieves are individuals each of whom tries to enforce control [torishimaru] as he pleases." Dan'atsu means to trample down on, suppress, curb, or crush. A more colloquial version of this compound, then, might be "clamping down on and snuffing out." Nihon Daijiten Kankōkai, ed., *Nihon Kokugo Daijiten*, 13:242, 15:68.

display of overly strong retaliation. It is only natural in wartime for spying and other destructive activities to be quelled by the occupying forces, but the Dutch had an unusually strong tendency to implicate and sacrifice natives in their stratagems. Of course this was not unreasonable since "in war all is fair,"[62] a truism which can probably be understood through comparison with the United States occupation of Japan. But Holland's case differed from Japan's because Holland would still have been part of the Allied forces even if she had met defeat. This difference was evident in the strategic activities on Java. But it is still incomprehensible that no criticism ever emerged of the Dutch military's responsibility for implicating ordinary civilians in its stratagems.

As we Java Kenpeitai continued to sentence to kikōsaku the ringleaders caught in the act of spying among those whom we had arrested, intelligence operatives attacked us relentlessly, although we continued to suppress and capture them. While these ceaseless attacks may reflect another weakness in the Japanese military occupation policy, it can also be said that by this point the Japanese forces may have already lost the strategic intelligence battles. And yet to have court-martialled all these criminals and carried out scrupulous trials for each of them would certainly have completely paralyzed the tactical army corps. Under the circumstances, the Java Kenpeitai alone cannot be blamed for implementing kikōsaku.

To us Kenpei, it was not the Indonesians but the Dutch whom we considered the enemy to the end. Indeed, which was it that provoked the strategic counterattacks by the various racial groups, excluding the Indonesians? Was it the incompetence of the Japanese military administration or the cleverness of the Dutch? The answer probably lies in both. It is the opinion of this association,[63] that the principal reason that the Dutch displayed such a vindictive attitude at the war crimes trials after the war, must be that they were well aware that they had sacrificed many natives in their military stratagems.

---

62 The saying "*Sensō to arebo, shudan o erande wa irarenai*" translates literally as "when it comes to war, one has not the choice to choose the means."

63 Zenkoku Kenyūkai Rengōkai.

THE SUMATRA KENPEITAI

The Kenpeitai Attached to Central and Northern Sumatra Operations

The first step in the assault on Sumatra was to occupy and secure the Palembang oil refineries without a single strategic error. The primary goal of the Greater East Asia War was to occupy the vital resource-rich regions of the Southern territories, making the securing of oil a supreme directive. In fact, more importance was placed on the occupation of Palembang than on the capture of Singapore, as is evident in the recollections of Southern Army Chief of Staff Colonel Arao Okinari. In order to ensure the success of the operation, the Palembang airport had first to be occupied by paratroop brigades to block enemy planes; then on February 15 the support of the Thirty-eighth Division (led by Lieutenant General Sakuno Tadayoshi) was enlisted for an upstream landing on the Telang, Musi, and Saleh Rivers. The aim was for the attack on Sumatra to begin immediately before the collapse of Singapore, because the fall of Singapore would surely be a clear warning to the enemy. As it turned out, however, the collapse of Singapore and the Thirty-eighth Division's landing operation in southern Sumatra took place on the same day.

The initial operation on Sumatra was a surprise parachute attack by the first air squadron. At noon on February 14 these "paratroop soldiers of the gods," now immortalized in song, leapt to a successful occupation of the Palembang airport and the areas adjacent to the oil refineries.

On February 20 the bulk of the division arrived in Palembang. Needless to say, Imperial Headquarters was pleased to learn of this flawless occupation of the oil fields. However the Kenpeitai had nothing much to do with this particular operation.

On February 19, the Southern Army Supreme Command officially announced the invasion of central and northern Sumatra and the Andaman archipelago by the Twenty-fifth Army Division. On March 12, the Imperial Guard[64] Division (led by Lieutenant General Nishimura Takuma) under the direction of the Twenty-fifth Army, landed with one subdivision on Kotaraja and Sabang Island in northern Sumatra, and the major portion of the division on Labuhanruku. Since the Dutch army had already unconditionally surrendered as of the ninth of March, the operation drew virtually no enemy resistance. The targets were Medan, Sumatra's main administrative center, and the important Padang area in the center of Sumatra's western shore. The operation was completed by March 17.

Under army orders, Army Lieutenant Colonel Ōishi Masahiko, Commander-in-Chief of the Twenty-fifth Army Kenpeitai, dispatched Lieutenant Colonel Yokota Masataka, chief of the provisional detachment, and his sixty Kenpei to assist with central and northern Sumatran operations.[65]

As planned, Lieutenant Colonel Yokota landed fifteen Kenpei led by First Lieutenant Gōshi Kōsuke[66] on Sabang Island off Kotaraja. Here they joined the Kobayashi branch unit (led by Major General Kobayashi Takashi), while the main provisional unit accompanied the Imperial Guard Division. The main force of the Kenpeitai landed with the major force of the [Thirty-eighth] division. While the military conducted its operations,

---

64 Konoe in Japanese.
65 The Kenpeitai unit on Sumatra was considered to be a "provisional detachment" until May of 1943, when its headquarters accompanied the Twenty-fifth Army headquarters in a move to Bukittinggi (*Gaishi*, p. 1130.)
66 Gōshi Kōsuke was a key figure in a series of massacres committed by the Kenpeitai in Singapore between February 18 and March 3, 1942, in which several thousand Chinese civilians were killed. See Russell, *Knights of Bushido*, p. 249. Captain Goshi was executed by the British in Kuala Lumpur in June 1947. (*Isho*, pp. 276, 623.)

the Kenpeitai enlisted the help of a fellow Japanese temporarily residing in Sumatra, a certain Mabuchi, known as the "Father of Aceh." With his help we made use of pro-Japanese elements to gather information, [1043] and be on the lookout for damaged bridges, telephone lines, and so on. Assuming primary responsibility for maintaining the military administration system, we turned our attention towards Medan.

Lieutenant Colonel Yokota had already been instructed by Imperial Guard Division Chief of Staff Colonel Obata Nobuyoshi that, following the invasion of Medan, we Kenpei were to take over the Dutch administrative system, intern the enemy people, and maintain law and order. Thus the first task to which we Kenpei gave careful thought was to get a good grip on the Dutch administrative system.

The greatest single mistake of the occupation administration up until this point had been the act of destroying in one blow the native administrative system, even before establishing a system to take its place. Those connected with the Kenpeitai who witnessed the government disregarding the language problem and the customs and ways of the native population, warned of the failure that had resulted from trampling on the ways of the past.[67] It seemed especially unnecessary because at the time there was little violent struggle in Sumatra, and the people were generally very warm towards the Japanese.[68]

At this point Lieutenant Colonel Yokota, influenced by the Kenpeitai, summoned Governor General Ott's[69] staff, just as it was configured at the time, to convene at the Medan Hotel. Governor Ott, the prefectural governors, the chief commissioner of the metropolitan police, and other department heads were there.

First, Lieutenant Colonel Yokota explained the policy of the military administration and so on, persuading them that it should be obeyed. Then he accompanied Governor Ott and the prefectural governors to

---

67 Like other military authorities, the Kenpeitai wanted to avoid repeating mistakes they had made in China. (Kanahele, "Japanese Occupation of Indonesia," p. 66.)
68 Only after the war did many Indonesians dare to express their feelings towards the Japanese army, and especially the Kenpeitai. "... With Japan's defeat, the Japanese army was suddenly hated by the people. Even the children scorned us," write the authors of *Gaishi*. The Kenpeitai rationalized this hostility, arguing that the Indonesians were disillusioned with the Japanese for giving in to the Allied side. (*Gaishi*, p. 1112.)
69 Although most definitely "Ott" in Japanese, the authors are presumably referring here to Sumatra Governor A. I. Spits.

the Governor's office where he issued the following orders: "From this day forth, general administration shall be carried out and law and order maintained as commanded by the Japanese army."

Those cooperating with the Japanese army and those used by the army were given arm bands with the red sun emblem. With the exception of high officials, the Dutch were interned in designated areas within Medan.

As for the police administration and all other commands, it was ordered that the chief commissioner of the metropolitan police be interned by the Kenpeitai, so that administrative affairs started off on a harmonious note. Having consulted and accepted counsel, we [the Kenpeitai] were mindful of conciliation with the native needs. Those used on the Dutch side were interned in five different places with their families and were permitted to move freely within the city. There was no need for them to receive any army supplies because they continued to receive their wages.

Three weeks after Medan was occupied, the military administration changed hands and Colonel Kurokawa assumed his new position in the administration. Subsequently we Kenpei returned to our original tasks of military policing, preventing espionage, and maintaining law and order. As part of our policy of maintaining law and order, we took measures towards conciliation with the native leaders, the Sultans. Namely, we Kenpei summoned them to explain [to them] Japanese army policy, after which they were administered a pledge of cooperation, or we Kenpei visited the Royal Palace, which reinforced their feelings of goodwill and empathy for the Japanese cause.

At the time the headquarters of the provisional Kenpeitai detachment were located in the Medan Tobacco Company building. First Lieutenant Hisamatsu was stationed with twenty of his Kenpei within the city to assist with the operations of the division, and gradually moved out to territories under Japanese control as the operations progressed.

[1044] When their operations drew to a close after the landing at Kotaraja, First Lieutenant Gōshi and his men in the Kobayashi branch unit contacted headquarters and were told to resume normal duties in the same area. From Kotaraja, they dispatched detachments to Bukittinggi, Sibolga,

Pakanbaru, and other areas where operations were being conducted.

The Southern Army ordered that southern Sumatra be included in the operational territories of the Twenty-fifth Army as of March 9. Lieutenant Colonel Yokota dispatched those under Second Lieutenant Ueno[70] to Palembang. Shortly afterwards, Ueno was replaced by the newly appointed Major Yamanouchi.

About two months later, around April 20, the Imperial Guard Division released the provisional Kenpeitai detachment and the detachment headquarters closed. The important officers in headquarters, including Lieutenant Colonel Yokota, returned to Singapore, while those under the unit commanders continued in their present capacity under the direct control of the Twenty-fifth Army Kenpeitai Commander-in-Chief Lieutenant Colonel Ōishi Masayuki. About this same time, the Imperial Guard Division command changed hands from First Lieutenant Nishimura to First Lieutenant Mutō Akira.

During this period[71] the Kenpeitai attached to the Imperial Guard Division accomplished the following:

1) The maintenance of law and order, especially the curbing of plundering by the natives.
2) The maintenance of order within the military, i.e. the control of illegal actions and looting by military men.
3) Religious policy, i.e. the correction of any misunderstanding regarding the native religion.
4) The arrest and internment of Governor Ott.
5) Forcing the Governor to order the surrender of the Dutch army (First Lieutenant Suzuki was largely responsible for this action).
6) Inspection of raw materials and the living conditions of the people with the use of the chief commissioner of the metropolitan police.

Note: Law and order were satisfactorily maintained immediately following initial operations on Sumatra. For example, on several occasions natives picked up drunk Japanese soldiers and took the trouble to deliver

---

70 Second Lieutenant Ueno was the combined Tokkō and Police Affairs chief of the first Kenpeitai unit on Sumatra. *(Gaishi,* p. 1132.)
71 March 22, 1942 through April 20, 1942, during which time the Kenpeitai provisional detachment was attached to the Imperial Guard Division.

them directly by car to the Kenpeitai. Except for the Chinese, the natives were extremely pro-Japanese.

At the time, the principal staff in this provisional Kenpeitai detachment were as follows:

> Provisional Detachment Commander—Kenpei Lieutenant Colonel Yokota Masataka
> Vice Commander—Kenpei First Lieutenant Suzuki Eikichi
> Attached—Kenpei First Lieutenant Gōshi Kōsuke
> Attached—Kenpei First Lieutenant Hisamatsu Haruyoshi
> Attached—Kenpei Second Lieutenant Ueno Ken'ichi
> Attached—Kenpei Chief Warrant Officer Hashimoto Kiichi
> Attached—Kenpei Chief Warrant Officer Tomomune Toshirō
> Attached—Kenpei Chief Warrant Officer Yamaguchi Kōichi

The Sumatra Kenpeitai

The provisional Kenpeitai detachment came into being in March 1942, in connection with the successful completion of central northern Sumatra operations. As operations progressed, we Kenpei were policing and maintaining law and order. Along with the move to Sumatra of the Twenty-fifth Army headquarters in May 1943 the Kenpeitai headquarters also moved to Bukittinggi, the seat of the military command.

In addition to assuming the military police duties of the Sumatran defense force, we Kenpei [1045] turned to suppressing the anti-Japanese overseas Chinese operations and investigating what remained of the Dutch army's spy network. We also handled, both shortly before and after the war, cases in which the Sumatran independence army seized weapons from our army.

The Central Sumatran Railway Crash

In August 1943 a train with over a dozen cars toppled off a central Sumatran railway (connecting Bukittinggi and Padang) bridge with a deafening roar. The bridge was located about one kilometer west of Pandang Panjang on the coast off the western sea. Over 500 people were killed and a great many were injured. The railway bridge spanned a shallow river some thirty meters wide. The first telegraph unit stationed in Padang Panjang mainly handled the incident with the cooperation of the local police. The majority of deaths were among the overseas Chinese and Minangkabau people; there were few injuries and no deaths among the Japanese passengers.

The Bukittinggi Kenpeitai unit formed a special investigative team of ten officers headed by a warrant officer; together with the local police it conducted on-the-spot investigations and tried to obtain information about the incident in the neighborhood. The investigation revealed that the accident had been caused by a snapped track on the bridge. In the year and some months since the start of the Japanese occupation, no repairs had been made on the tracks and this had taken a heavy toll. We Kenpei covered the area in which the incident had taken place, carefully retracing the movements of people in the neighborhood on the days before and after the incident, but were unable to identify any suspicious characters. There was absolutely no suspicion that the accident had been a plot. Thus we Kenpei who investigated the data announced our conclusion that "a break in the tracks was the result of unsatisfactory upkeep," thereby terminating the investigation into the incident.

The Aborted Insurgence of the Dutch Army Commander of Sumatra

Major General Overakker, the Dutch Army Commander for Sumatra, was interned in a concentration camp in Medan. Towards the end of 1942, he began expecting an Allied counteroffensive, and was using the shopkeepers and others who serviced the camp to maintain contact with the outside world.

The General was planning to direct the army once it landed at the time of the Allied counteroffensive, and planning the organization of the spy squads that would cause disturbances to the Japanese army. He was diligently expanding and strengthening the anti-Japanese organization throughout all of Sumatra. He had put to work all the overseas Chinese connected with the Dutch and former property-owning Dutch soldiers being used by the Japanese army. Since the middle of 1943, he had been secretly contacting parachute spies landing by bomber plane and spies sneaking in by submarine, and using the war funds provided to the spies, such as gold coins and counterfeit notes, to expand the organization.

At the end of 1942 the Kenpei under First Lieutenant Hisamatsu Haruyoshi, [1046] commander of the Special Operations Division in the Sumatra Kenpeitai headquarters, received news that enemy spies had infiltrated deep into the Takegon mountains of Aceh province in northern Sumatra. Through the capture and subsequent investigation of Dutch Army Captain Van de Tjark in early March 1943, we confirmed that an underground organization had indeed spread throughout Sumatra.

Kenpeitai Commander-in-Chief Colonel Hirano Toyoji thought this news very important. He immediately ordered our units to spy on this underground organization. The operation was called "Operation Su."[72] We delved full-force into the investigation, and approximately half a year later finally exposed the entire organization. We then prepared to move.

On September 20, 1943, the Sumatra Kenpeitai headquarters and our units undertook a wholesale arrest. We arrested 160 suspects, and seized a considerable amount of ammunition, arms, and clothing.

The principals arrested in this incident are as follows:

The Ringleaders:

Dutch Supreme Commander for Sumatra—Major General Overakker

---

72 "Su" and "Ka" are equivalent to letters in the Japanese phonetic alphabet. "Operation Su" and "Operation Ka," described later in this text, are considered by the Zenkenren to be the "two major incidents in the history of the Sumatra Kenpeitai." Kenpeitai Commander-in-Chief Hirano Toyoji, the architect of both counterespionage schemes, committed suicide on September 20, 1945 in anticipation of having to stand trial for his actions. The Dutch held all the successive commanders of the Kotaraja Kenpei unit liable for both operations in the war crimes trials. *[Gaishi,* p. 1134.)

(Death sentence)
Northern Commander—Colonel Gosenson[73] (Death sentence)
Brigade members—Captain Van de Tjark (Acquitted)
First Lieutenant Surell[74] (Acquitted)

Of the some 160 people arrested, about seventy cases were dispatched to martial law proceedings[75] based on criminal actions clarified during the investigations. As a result of the trial, Major General Overakker and those under him were sentenced to death. The executions were carried out by order of the Minister of the Army in May 1945.[76]

This case was handled by the special operations unit in headquarters and the Medan, Kotaraja, and Palembang units.

The Theft of Army Notes from the Post Office

In the latter part of November 1943 500,000 yen worth of military currency was stolen from the Jambi Post Office in Sumatra. Immediately following this incident another 100,000 yen were stolen from the Special Muaratebo Post Office. The police had little concrete evidence that the suspects they had arrested and interrogated in the Jambi case had done anything wrong. What little evidence they had was very weak. We therefore suspected that the police had not yet found the real criminals.

A month after the incident occurred, the Twenty-fifth Army Commander-in-Chief Lieutenant General Tanabe Moritake learned of an upcoming tour by the Southern Army Supreme Chief of Staff Major General Yahagi. He ordered the Kenpeitai Commander-in-Chief to arrest the real criminals immediately to preserve the honor of the military administration. Kenpeitai Commander-in-Chief Colonel Hirano received these strict orders and immediately designated ten Kenpei under First Lieutenant Hayashi Asao, chief of the headquarters' police affairs

---

73 Hōsenson in *rōmaji*.
74 Sureru in *rōmaji*.
75 Gunritsu kaigi ni jiken-sōchi shita.
76 Minister of the Army is *Rikugun Daijin* in Japanese. "Major General Overakker and Colonel Gosenson were confined in a farmhouse until the end of 1944. In May of 1945, with the news that the Allied landing was approaching, the military command ordered their execution by the Kenpeitai." (*Gaishi*, p. 1148).

division, to take charge of the investigation under the direction of the chief of the detachment.

[1047] First Lieutenant Kenpei Hayashi and his men began the investigation on December 25, 1943. They soon concluded that the real culprits were from the telephone bureau, the rival institution of the Jambi Post Office. They were the head of the bureau, who was a native, his younger brother, and three employees of the bureau. We arrested them and presented considerable supporting evidence. It was now clear to us that the suspects arrested by the police were not the true criminals, so they were immediately released.

We discovered next that the culprits in the Muaretebo case were local employees of the Muaretebo bureau, and bore no relation to the Jambi case. We arrested these four also, and our investigation confirmed that they were indeed the real criminals. Their cases were dispatched to martial law proceedings.[77]

Not only was the Japanese military administration able to preserve its dignity in this case, but we Kenpei gave a splendid show of our investigative abilities to the military police authorities as we resolved the entire problem within only fifteen days of beginning the investigation.

The Wholesale Arrest of Anti-Japanese Chiang Kai-Shek Sympathizers

The anti-Japanese overseas Chinese in Singapore had instigated an anti-Japanese movement among overseas Chinese throughout the entire Southern region even prior to the Greater East Asia War. They had succeeded in amassing vast sums of capital to support their cause and send to their Chongqing government, and their strong organization existed even in Sumatra.

Starting in early 1943, the organization had geared up again, and an important man in the Chongqing National Government, Zhao Lian, had infiltrated into central Sumatra and instigated the movement. Having learned about the resurgence of this underground organization in mid-December 1943, Kenpeitai Commander-in-Chief Colonel Hirano Toyoji marshalled all his units to mobilize a wholesale roundup of organization

---

77 In the original text, *gunritsu kaigi ni jiken-sōchi shita.*

members. The effort was called "Operation Ka" and was considered to be very important. We arrested 120 overseas Chinese. After the investigations, about thirty people who had clearly committed crimes were dispatched to martial law proceedings.[78]

None of those arrested turned out to be the big shots whom we had hoped for, however, and we could not prove the existence of a definite organization. We failed to arrest the man recognized as the ringleader of this movement, Zhao Lian, who had found out about the roundup early and fled.

The Palembang Army Hospital Director Scandal

Army physician Colonel Kitazawa Yoshitaka took over the position of director of the Palembang Hospital in Sumatra in June 1944. Ever since his arrival, he had been prone to illness. Confined to his sickbed, he had summoned live-in nurses from the hospital to attend to him in the billet one at a time. In due course he proceeded to abuse the nurses. He had actually abused five nurses, none of whom had ever spoken up for fear of retaliation because he was the director of the hospital.

[1048] Coincidentally, a certain Lance Corporal Kotani from Yamanishi prefecture, who was an influential politician in his hometown and had worked for the Imperial Rule Assistance Association[79] before enlisting, was on close terms with the nurses. Kotani was suspicious of the director, who continued to employ the nurses even though he was not seriously ill. He confirmed his suspicions of abuse through one of the nurses. While the story was being leaked to the relaying Kenpeitai, word of the slander spread within the hospital to Kotani's colleagues and to other employees.

Palembang unit commander Major Yamane received the report on this case from the Kenpeitai, and initiated a top-secret investigation. However, he was transferred to another position before he could confirm

---

78 *Gunritsu kaigi ni jiken sōchi-shita.*
79 The Imperial Rule Assistance Association [*Taisei Yokusan-kai*] was formed by konoe and comprised of former Diet leaders. Under Prime Minister Tōjo, it supported and helped to consolidate Tōjo's party. See F. C. Jones, *Japan's New Order in Asia: Its Rise and Fall, 1937-45* (London: Oxford University Press, 1954), pp. 420-21, and Benda, *Crescent and the Rising Sun*, p. 265, n. 20.

the incident, and the matter was left pending.

The new Palembang unit commander, Major Yokoyama Kentarō, ordered the judicial chief[80] to resume the investigation in early February 1945. Yokoyama could hardly permit a commanding officer of such high standing to get away with such an offense.

On his round to the Palembang unit, Kenpeitai Commander-in-Chief Hirano told Major Yokoyama that he shared the opinion of Colonel Furukawa, chief of the martial law department, who felt that only moderate action should be taken under the circumstances, since it is always difficult in such situations to distinguish between real abuse and mutual consent. He also feared that if too much were made of the incident, military discipline in similar situations might be too much of a problem. Major Yokoyama respected his superior, Commander-in-Chief Colonel Hirano Toyoji, but his sense of justice prevailed. Yokoyama believed there was sufficient evidence of abuse and that a judicial punishment should be meted out, for such immorality certainly was unacceptable in such a high-ranking military man.

Before long Furukawa, chief of the martial law department, was transferred to Taiwan and was replaced by Lieutenant Colonel Nagabuchi Yoshio, who came to Palembang from Bukittinggi. Major Yokoyama paid a call on Lieutenant Colonel Nagabuchi to make an appeal for those involved in the incident. In this conference, they decided to bring the matter to court martial,[81] even if it meant risking their jobs.

Lance Corporal Kotani of the army hospital was an in-law of the wife of Prime Minister Tōjō, and had secretly reported this incident in a letter to her. Prime Minister Tōjō had learned about this and inquired about the incident in a telegram to Twenty-fifth Army Commander Lieutenant General Tanabe. Once this had happened, Lieutenant General Tanabe could no longer ignore the incident, and the affair was immediately brought before a court martial.[82]

Once the incident came to trial and one of the nurses had testified concerning the intent of the accused, Yokoyama won over the cooperation of two or three other nurses who had deliberately decided to obfuscate

---

80 *Shihō shunin* in Japanese.
81 *Gunpō kaigi.*
82 Gunpō kaigi.

the incident to protect their future. The nurses testified as witnesses.

Hospital director Kitazawa argued that when Major Yokoyama had once visited the hospital to ask him about the rumor of violations, he had denied the rumor. He insisted that even if such a thing had happened, it would have been because of the nurses' consent, so that there was no reason for the Kenpeitai to interfere in the matter.

After this the public prosecutor's office undertook a direct examination of the case in question. The Kenpeitai received directions from the public prosecutor's office to assist in the incident. As we gathered evidence and the investigation proceeded, [1049] we discovered that the hospital director had committed improprieties with the war relief funds. Written documents concerning these and other instances of misconduct were sent to the court martial by early March 1945.

We Kenpei deliberated over whether or not there was intent in this case. The issue should be treated no differently in this instance than in society at large. Also, because all of the victims were unmarried nurses, their cases could all be narrowed down to one person.

The court martial trial began in the Bukittinggi courts towards the end of April 1945. Presiding were the judge, Army Chief of Staff Second Lieutenant Tanihagi Hanao, and two commissioned officers of the court. The public prosecutors were also present. The defendant claimed that there had been mutual consent from beginning to end, while the victimized nurse insisted to the end that she had been abused.

The court's decision was for three years' penal servitude, lowering of rank, and revocation of the defendant's medical license. The defendant was sent off to the Kurume Army Garrison Prison[83] and was released after the end of the war.

The court completely forbade any audience at the hearing. The audience consisted of Major Yokoyama and an army physician. The public prosecutor investigated Lance Corporal Kitani for slandering a senior authority, but treated his case as a minor offense. As for the nurse, she was sent back to her hometown in Yamagata Prefecture.

At the time, there was a strong feeling among the higher-ranking officers that the Kenpeitai should not have been involved to such a degree.

---

83 Located in Fukuoka prefecture in Japan.

But those of us in charge of maintaining military discipline believed there was no question but that the incident should not have been overlooked. In the army the higher-ranking officers always have advantages over the lower-ranking officers, but at the same time their responsibilities should be heavier. We Kenpei could certainly not have kept quiet about this case, if only because the doctor took advantage of the hierarchy existing between himself and the nurse.

[1220] TERMINATION OF THE WAR AND THE JAVA KENPEITAI

On May 24, 1945, the Seventh District Division of the Army issued the following order to the Sixteenth Army of Java: "Upon the enemy offensive, you must gradually weaken enemy strength everywhere and use your utmost force to crush their plan. Every effort must be made to secure the strategic areas of western Java as the circumstances compel it." The Sixteenth [1221] Army thus made plans to reinforce the major resistance encampments in the high plains around Bandung, build guerrilla bases, and shift to strategic combat training for the men and officers. Even up to this point the Allied air and naval forces had been overwhelming—conditions were such that our coastal encampments would inevitably be thrashed. Under the circumstances it was imperative for the Sixteenth Army to establish strong bases in the mountains and other remote areas, for our only hope was the battle on land. By early June the location of the bases had been decided upon, and construction began. Soon August was before us.

On August 12, the Sixteenth Army Command in Batavia learned in utter amazement that the Japanese government had accepted the Potsdam Declaration. For the army command, the most painful aspect of the surrender was that the Southern Army had already promised independence to the Indonesian volunteer army. Army Commander-in-Chief Lieutenant General Nagano Yuichirō immediately assembled the Chief of Staff Major General Yamamoto Moichirō's staff in an emergency conference. He decided to withhold the news of the surrender for the time being, before it actually took place. He did this because he was worried about the possibility of an insurrection by the Indonesian volunteer army. He wanted to eke out even a little time to take measures to maintain law and order after the surrender.

Kenpeitai Commander-in-Chief Major General Nishida Shōzō received the order from the army command. He immediately directed Captain Iizuka Kinjirō of the Batavia Tokkō division to communicate the army commander's order to the unit commanders in every region. Captain Iizuka first looked up the times at which the train would stop at each station before Surabaya, and then telegrammed the commanders of each unit to let them know when to stand by at the station. This way the Captain was able to transmit the order to each unit leader at the respective station platform, as he headed by train toward the Surabaya unit. He returned to Batavia on the evening of August 14.

The next day everyone gathered even in the Sixteenth Army headquarters to listen attentively to the Emperor's broadcast of the imperial edict. The following day, August 16, the Sixteenth Army convened a staff officers' meeting and decided reverently to obey the imperial edict.[84] Army Commander-in-Chief Nagano was concerned about possible disruptions by the Indonesian volunteer army and disturbances of the public peace. He gave strict orders to each Kenpei unit to uphold law and order. However, as noted above, the Southern Army Supreme Command had already granted independence to the two leaders of the Indonesian volunteer army: Sukarno (later President), whose homecoming had just been celebrated in Jakarta[85] on August 14, and Hatta. Before dawn on August 16, Sukarno and Hatta were suddenly kidnapped by extremists in the volunteer army. Now that the leaders had been taken by force, an armed uprising by the high-spirited volunteer army was inevitable. The Army Command immediately ordered the Kenpeitai to extricate Sukarno.

To obtain information on Sukarno, the Kenpeitai headquarters used primarily Tokkō division chief Captain Iizuka Kinjirō, but even resorted to using the radio-probe squads. Unfortunately however his whereabouts remained unclear. Sukarno and Hatta had been taken to some volunteer army barracks in Rengasdengklok, some eighty kilometers east of Jakarta. Then, on the night of August 16, under pressure from the extremist faction in the volunteer army, Sukarno and Hatta had returned to Jakarta and

---

84 In Sumatra, three Kenpeitai units and several groups of Kenpei resisted surrender. Others committed suicide upon hearing the news. (*Gaishi*, p. 1147.)
85 Still known as Batavia during the Japanese occupation.

negotiated the pronouncement of a declaration of independence with the central military administration.

Even Rear Admiral Maeda Tadashi of the Naval Office [1 2 2 2] secretly cooperated in the matter of Sukarno. That evening Sukarno and Hatta had met with Nishimura, chief of the General Affairs Division of the central military administration, to demand approval of the declaration of independence, and the immediate convening of an independent committee for the preparation of independence. Major General Nishimura had refused them, explaining that "Now that the war has terminated and we have the responsibility for maintaining the present state of affairs with respect to the Allied armies, I cannot possibly formally authorize this without orders from central command." At that point Sukarno and Hatta returned to the official residence of Rear Admiral Maeda, who was sympathetic to the independence movement, and on the morning of August 17 drafted their proclamation of independence.

On the next day, August 18, the Committee for the Preparation of Independence convened. The committee agreed on a provisional constitution, which had been drafted earlier, and approved the assumption of the office of the president by Sukarno. What we would like to point out here is that, like Rear Admiral Major General Maeda, the army and the Kenpeitai also favored independence for Indonesia, and also wanted to render assistance if we could.[86] The Kenpeitai was also vaguely aware that Navy Major General Maeda was contributing to the independence movement. However, we were under orders from the Southern Army Supreme Command to turn over all arms to the occupying British and Dutch armies. Thus, until this task was accomplished, the army's mission was to preserve peace and order. If the volunteer army were to revolt, we would have to suppress them, no matter how nasty it might be.

Nonetheless, the independence movement inevitably wanted weapons, and saw this as an ideal opportunity to expand its power. They had their eyes on the ammunition magazines, the smaller stationed units, and the Kenpeitai. The volunteer armies attacked those stationed units in great

---

86 There is little evidence to suggest the Kenpeitai were truly committed to the cause of independence. For instance Kanahele points out that "Perhaps more than any other group in the Japanese military administration, the Kenpeitai betrayed the most exaggerated fears of Putera's capacity to stir up nationalist excitement." (Kanahele, "Japanese Occupation of Indonesia," p. 76.)

force. If our units had only calmly turned over their weapons, nothing would have happened,[87] but the units refused, resulting in a tragedy in which they were all massacred. As a matter of fact, Second Lieutenant Odamura Genzō and his twelve men in the small Madiun detachment were all slaughtered.

Reverently obeying the imperial edict, the Sixteenth Army found itself caught in a dilemma between following orders from on high and the independence movement. This unfortunately led to many men being sacrificed after the surrender.[88]

On September 15, a high-spirited Sukarno announced the declaration of independence before a crowd of 60,000 gathered in Batavia's Gambir Plaza.[89] The Kenpeitai tried to do something to stop Sukarno, who had arrived guarded by the volunteer army, but we were cut off by Lieutenant Colonel Miyamoto, an army staff officer.

On September 18, an Allied advance force landed in Jakarta. On the 25th, the British army landed, and on September 27 occupation by the principal Allied forces began. After this, the volunteer armies broke into revolt everywhere, and began fighting with the British and Dutch armies. Tragically, the Sixteenth Army became embroiled in all of this.

On November 3, all members of the Sixteenth Army assembled in Batavia and did what they could to survive on their own, as they awaited orders from the Allied armies. [1223] The Kenpeitai especially was used to suppress the Indonesian independence movement,[90] a fact which was tragically magnified at the end in the vengeful war crimes trials. As we mentioned before, the Java Kenpeitai became embroiled in the Indonesian

---

87 It was in the interest of the Kenpeitai to cooperate with the volunteer armies. As the *Gaishi* points out, "If we Kenpei were to come face to face with the people, the general Japanese populace would be moaning in pain throughout the land, and it would mean real trouble." (*Gaishi*, p. 1116.)

88 By the end of the war about 100 Kenpei, mostly in the smaller units, had been killed by Indonesians. (*Gaishi*, p. 1126.) After the war, the Japanese army lost 1,057 men, 544 of whom were killed in action. (Ibid., p. 1129.) The smaller Kenpeitai units continued to suffer the most. Many Kenpei deeply resented being used by the Allied armies to suppress the Indonesian people after the war. (Ibid., pp. 1125-26.)

89 On August 17, the date of the original proclamation of independence, Sukarno avoided using Gambir Plaza, so as not to clash with Japanese troops. Therefore the reference to September 15 here is possibly to the massive rally held on September 19 in Ikada Square (now known as Medan Merdeka). For an account of this, see Anderson, *Java in a Time of Revolution*, pp. 119-24.

90 In the words of Sergeant Major Ishida, the Kenpei felt it their duty to "resolutely take up the challenge of blasting apart the radical elements in the independence movement." (*Gaishi*, p. 1116.)

independence struggle at the war's end, and sacrificed a great many. Here we shall simply summarize the situation of each unit.

As for the Jakarta (formerly Batavia) unit, the British army advance party immediately arrested commander Major Chō Kōnosuke as a war crimes suspect.[91] Thereafter, Captain Iizuka Kinjirō commanded the unit.

On January 3, 1946 the Jakarta unit was disarmed in Bogor city. All members were immediately placed in custody as war crimes suspects in Glodok prison in Jakarta.[92]

During the seventy-five days following the end of the war we kept our distress over the defeat to ourselves, and fulfilled our duty to maintain peace and order and suppress the dangerous rioters. During this time, two auxiliary Kenpei were sacrificed.

The independence volunteer army surrounded our Surakarta unit at the end of the war, but our unit commander refused to hand over our weapons. The situation immediately exploded into a battle, and three Kenpei were shot. We men knew there was a danger that we would all be killed if the battle continued, so we persuaded our commander Captain Satō Hyōkichi to turn over our weapons to the volunteer army. We were all taken into custody in Solo prison.[93] Two auxiliary Kenpei died from illness while we were in prison.[94]

In the Madiun detachment, commander Second Lieutenant Odamura Genzō and eleven Kenpei were all massacred, as noted earlier.[95]

---

91 Chō Kōnosuke was executed in Glodok Prison on December 30, 1947. In a letter written to his mother the day he received his death sentence, he speaks of "having the confidence to be able to say that I have lived by love." (*Isho*, pp. 376-78.)
92 Seven Batavia Kenpei, including unit commander Chō, were sentenced to death, and twenty-three received prison terms. (*Isho*, p. 377.)
93 During the confrontation with the mob of volunteer fighters, one Kenpei who had tried earlier to persuade his commander not to resort to violence, ran out "in a rain of bullets," waving a white flag on his pistol and calling for surrender, in defiance of his commander's orders. The crowd ceased fire at once. The Kenpei unit then negotiated among themselves before surrendering to the volunteer army. This incident is described in detail in *Gaishi*, pp. 1116-17.
94 "The Kenpei imprisoned in Solo jail inside the city were loathed by the city people. The people had their revenge with the food they gave us. Conditions were miserable. The Kenpeitai prisoners had one egg and one rotten banana for every two men each day. Instead of tea there was mosquito larvae-infested water. The main meal consisted of two sweet potatoes. Because of this, two assistant Kenpei died within two short months of being imprisoned, and others became sick with tuberculosis or starvation. The Surakarta unit was diminishing again." (*Gaishi*, p. 1117.)
95 The figures in the text are contradictory on this point. On page 61 (page 1222 of the original), the authors indicate that Oda-mura and twelve Kenpei were slaughtered.

The Indonesian volunteer army imprisoned Semarang Kenpei unit commander Wada Kunishige and more than twenty of his Kenpei. But Japanese in the army transport bureau came to the rescue and, after a battle, succeeded in capturing the prison. Forty Japanese in the prison had already been massacred, but they rescued thirty survivors and about a dozen Dutch. After rescuing two other Japanese and several Dutch in another prison, we reached reconciliation with the volunteer army.

In Pekalongan province near Tegal, Chief Warrant Officer Hoshino Katsushige's pacification efforts and management at the end of the war had been most appropriate. The natives had not even caused the slightest disruption, and had good feelings toward the Kenpei. When we left, they gave us a farewell party.[96] They even provided a guarded train for us to travel to our assembly area in; this was very rare.

The Kediri unit assembled in the Watts [?][97] coffee plantation in Kediri prefecture, but was seized by the volunteer army, disarmed, and interned in the Badilok [?][98] sugar factory in Kediri. We were made to live under the worst conditions without supplies. Next, we were moved to Toloagon [?] prison where we joined the Surabaya unit. The Surabaya unit maintained law and order in the Surabaya district after the war as ordered by the Allied armies. In early September, the volunteer army had resisted the coming of the Allied occupation armies, believing that they would obstruct independence. It attacked the Allied army barracks, and in October blew up the Amal powder magazine on Mao island which led to a violent battle with the British and Dutch armies. In the midst of this maelstrom, the unit was disarmed and sent, guarded by the Indonesian army, to Toloagon prison in Kediri state.

In February 1946 we left Pontianak harbor for the [1224] Riau archipelago, where the Southern Army was assembling. From there, we were all taken into custody as war crimes suspects and interned in Singapore's Changi prison.

---

96 This scene recalls the send-off the Kenpei claim to have received on December 24, 1949, the day those who were serving sentences for war crimes left Batavia harbor for Japan. In the words of the ex-Kenpei: "That day many higher-ups in the Indonesian government of the new president Sukarno, who had won independence, turned out in great numbers to see the Japanese war criminals off and to thank them." *(Gaishi,* p. 1159.)
97 Wattasu in *rōmaji.*
98 Baderoku in *rōmaji.*

Because it did not yield to the independence army's stubborn demand for weapons, our Surabaya wharf detachment was attacked in early October, but was saved through the efforts of the Navy Harbor Office. The detachment escaped by boat and, after throwing its ammunition overboard, was reunited with the Surabaya unit. Chō Keiyo,[99] a Taiwanese interpreter, was killed during this episode by the independence army.

Our Bandung unit also assumed responsibility for maintaining law and order after the end of the war. The Indonesian volunteer army began attacking the Japanese army platoons in the Bandung area to get hold of weapons to expand its power. In late September it suddenly attacked the Japanese army sanitorium in Garut,[100] and Warrant Officer Fukuda of the Medical Department and ten of his men were killed. The volunteer army also often attacked Kenpei who were guarding Allied army commissioned officers and other important people.

On October 10th a group of volunteer armies attacked the Bandung Kenpei unit in one fell swoop to obtain weapons, but we Kenpei fought back and repelled the attack in two hours.

In late November, the Allied army disarmed the Bandung unit and incarcerated the Kenpei in Jakarta's Glodok prison.

The Purwokerto unit also attempted to guard the civil peace after the war, but the independence movement was violent and the Japanese army had moved elsewhere, so the unit primarily engaged in farming. The Purwokerto area was generally tranquil, and there were no Japanese casualties. Around May 1946, the unit left Java, guarded by the local volunteer army, and headed for Singapore.

The Serang unit was surrounded and attacked by a native mob, but suffered no casualties and was able to withdraw to Batavia. As mentioned above, the majority of the Java Kenpei was incarcerated as war crimes suspects.

The Kenpei from every unit in eastern Java left Java towards the end of 1945 or first half of 1946. Extremely few of the demobilized Kenpei went directly back to the homeland. Just about everyone was incarcerated in

---

99 Zhang Qingyu in Chinese.
100 Garu in *rōmaji*.

Changi prison in Singapore. Then, towards the end of 1946, most victims were transferred on the basis of interrogations to Cipinan prison on the outskirts of Batavia, where we underwent war crimes trials.

[1225] THE TWENTY-FIFTH ARMY KENPEITAI AND MAJOR GENERAL HIRANO

Major General Hirano Toyoji, Commander-in-Chief of the Twenty-fifth Army Kenpeitai, arrived at his post in Singapore in March of 1943. When the Twenty-fifth Army Headquarters was moved to Bukittinggi in Sumatra, he was also transferred there as Commanding Officer of the Sumatra Kenpeitai, and was in charge of collecting intelligence, maintaining civil peace, and order within the army. His most notable accomplishments were "Operation Su" and "Operation Ka."[101]

When Japan met defeat on August 15, 1945, the Major General, unable to bear the fact that his subordinates would be convicted as war criminals for incidents that he himself had directed, and unwilling to be incarcerated himself as a war crime suspect, resolved to assume responsibility for the defeat and in his quarters calmly committed suicide. In his final moments he was completely composed like an old-fashioned samurai. All those in the military command deeply trusted the General. He was a great officer, deeply revered by his subordinates for his integrity of character.

In the middle of October 1945, the volunteer army in Tarutung province seized a lot of military equipment and ammunition from the local police department. The chief provincial official immediately demanded that the Kenpeitai unit commanders and the garrison[102] commander handle the incident. Captain Hayashi Asao, the Sibolga Kenpei unit leader, promptly conferred with the garrison leader, who insisted on using force to recapture the arms. Captain Hayashi explained that it would be disadvantageous to

---
101 See chapter on Sumatra Kenpeitai above.
102 *Keibichūtai* in Japanese.

work with troops who no longer had any fighting spirit and, now that the war was over, he was requesting the Kenpei to take charge. The Captain then returned to his unit.

The next morning he went to the volunteer army barracks with a dozen or more of his men, and was able to persuade the local commander to turn over the stolen weapons. He was able to confiscate two truckloads full of equipment, ammunition, and other goods.

Later, after the war was over, a native army known as the Independence volunteer army[103] was organized in Sibolga in Sumatra. The army expanded gradually, plundering weapons, ammunition, and other resources in Japanese custody on an almost daily basis.

One day the local volunteer army suddenly kidnapped Colonel Okada Tetsuo, commander of the Sibolga garrison, and blockaded the Kenpei unit. The scheme was to plunder the equipment and ammunition in Japanese custody without causing any bloodshed.

In January of 1946, a hundred and forty or so members of the local volunteer army approached the unit commander's quarters, randomly firing their light machine-guns and waving their spears and barbarian swords. We Kenpei had gotten wind of the attack earlier and took advantage of our knowledge to make a sortie on the volunteer army. With the cooperation of the garrison, which arrived thirty minutes later, we succeeded in capturing about a hundred volunteer soldiers and rebuffed the others.

Since the war had terminated, we turned the prisoners over to the local police for management. This was the best thing to do from the standpoint of maintaining civil order.

As mentioned above, the Kenpei were assigned along with the stationed units to maintaining peace and order until the Allied army arrived. But during this period there were some Kenpei who would not willingly be seized as war criminals, and left their units to join the Indonesian independence armies. [1226] All of us other Kenpei were then interned as war crimes suspects in Medan prison towards the end of 1945 or thereafter. We were all interrogated and, in a severe judgment, a great many Kenpei fell victim.

---

103 *Dokuritsu giyūgun*

About thirty Sumatra Kenpei of warrant officer or lesser rank, who were unwilling to be incarcerated as war crimes suspects after the war, left their units and joined the Indonesian war for independence, as mentioned above. After the war for independence they managed to overcome countless dangers and difficulties, and survived to take Indonesian citizenship, and find various forms of employment. We have verified at least seven former Kenpei, all of whom have assumed leadership roles in the community.

It can also be presumed that many died in the struggle for Indonesian independence, along with the seventy or so other military men from other units who died in the independence struggle. We have identified at least twelve of the Kenpei who are buried near Bukittinggi on the western coast, whose distinguished service has been recognized by the Indonesian government.[104]

---

104 The *Gaishi* notes that the Indonesian government holds a memorial service every year for the Japanese soldiers who died in the war for independence. *(Gaishi,* p. 1160.)

[1294] THE SPECIFIC CHARACTER OF THE DUTCH WAR CRIMES TRIALS

When looking at the war crimes trials in the Netherlands East Indies, we should keep in mind that after the war the Indonesian independence army revolted in every district and Holland's army got scorched trying to suppress it. Ultimately the Dutch were unable to suppress the Indonesians and ended up granting independence.

However, in the interim, the war crimes trials were being held. The Dutch authorities insisted that the Japanese army had assisted in the independence movement. Our arrested criminals were blamed with hatred for Holland's own decline, and there was no attempt to disguise this bias in the trials. Thus the trial became a cruel, even reckless, reprisal trial, and there were many of us who fought back tears as we brooked the unfounded insults.

Looking back on world history, Holland was once a champion of the aggressor nations. Of the many Dutch colonies, the Netherlands East Indies occupied an extremely important position economically. One has only to look at the natural resource oil, as one example, for it to be very clear what sort of economic role Indonesia shouldered for Holland's prosperity.

It is also an historical fact that Indonesia took advantage of the end of the Greater East Asia War to gain independence. However, another fact which cannot be denied is that one group of soldiers in the Japanese army did side with the Indonesian independence movement. It may be quite natural then for Holland—which sacrificed the lives of many Dutch soldiers and a large budget as a result of the Indonesian revolt for independence, and then lost its greatest colony when the colony became independent—to hate the Japanese army. But that is a different problem of altogether another dimension from that of those convicted at the war crimes trials.

Luckily for Holland, she was in a victor's position. The Dutch designated [1295] as many as 1,033 war criminals, of whom 389 were Kenpei war criminals.[105] The number sentenced to death reached 85 men, and there were more Kenpei victims than in other regions. These are the realities of the Netherlands East Indies war crimes trials.

---

105 These are total figures for all the Dutch trials in Batavia, Medan, Tanjungpinang, Pontianak, Banjarmasin, Balikpapan, Makasar, Kupang, Ambon, Manado, Porranja [?], and Morotai. There were 199 Kenpei convicted in the Java trials, and 55 Kenpei convicted in the Sumatra trials. *(Seishi,* p. 1323.)

BIBLIOGRAPHY

English

Ames, Walter L. *Police and Community in Japan.* Berkeley: University of California Press, 1981.

Anderson, Benedict Richard O'Gorman. *Java in a Time of Revolution, Occupation and Resistance, 1944-46.* Ithaca: Cornell University Press, 1972.

_____. *Some Aspects of Indonesian Politics under the Japanese Occupation: 1944-45.* Ithaca: Cornell Modern Indonesia Project, 1961.

Azis, M. A. *Japan's Colonialism and Indonesia.* The Hague: Martinus Nijhoff, 1955.

Benda, Harry J. *The Crescent and the Rising Sun: Indonesian Islam Under the Japanese Occupation, 1942-45.* The Hague: Van Hoeve, 1958.

Benda, Harry J.; Irikura, James K.; and Kishi, Koichi. *Japanese Military Administration in Indonesia: Selected Documents.* New Haven: Yale University Press, 1965.

Bertram, James M. *Beneath the Shadow: A New Zealander in the Far East 1939-46.* New York: The John Day Company, 1947, pp. 103-125. (Hong Kong.)

Butow, Robert J. C. *Tojo and the Coming of War.* Berkeley: University of

California Press, 1961, pp. 72-73, 89, 115.

Brooks, Lester. *Behind Japan's Surrender: The Secret Struggle that Ended an Empire.* New York: McGraw-Hill Book Co., 1968.

Chin, Kee Onn. *Malaya Upside Down.* 2d ed., Singapore: Jitts and Co., 1946. (Malaya).

Dahm, Bernhard. "The Japanese Interregnum, 1942-45." In *History of Indonesia in the Twentieth Century.* Translated by P. S. Falla. New York: Praeger Publishers, 1971.

Dew, Gwen. *Prisoner of the Japs.* New York: Alfred A. Knopf. 1943. (Hong Kong.)

Dower, John W., ed. *Origins of the Modern Japanese State: Selected Writings of E. H. Norman.* New York: Pantheon Books, 1975.

Elsbree, W. H. *Japan's Role in Southeast Asian Nationalist Movements, 1940-45.* Cambridge, Mass.: Harvard University Press, 1953.

Fairbank, John K.; Reischauer, Edwin D.; and Craig, Albert M. *East Asia: Tradition and Transformation.* 2d ed. Cambridge, Mass.: Harvard University Press, 1978.

Fujiwara, Lieutenant General Iwaichi. *F Kikan: Japanese Army Intelligence Operations in Southeast Asia During World War II.* Translated by Akashi Yoji. Hong Kong: Heinemann Asia, 1983.

Goodell, Stephen. "Song of Survival: A Film Documentary." Paper presented at Washington and Southeast Regional Seminar on Japan, 22 September 1984, University of Maryland, College Park. Mimeographed.

Goto, Kenichi. "Japanese Reactions in 1945 Indonesia." Tokyo: Waseda University. Paper read at Annual Meeting of the Association of Asian Studies, 1984, in Washington, D.C. Mimeographed.

Guillain, Robert. *I Saw Tokyo Burning: An Eyewitness Narrative from Pearl Harbor to Hiroshima*. Translated by William Byron. Garden City: Doubleday and Company, 1981, pp. 67-69, 161-63, 214-20.

Hall, John W. and Toyoda, Takeshi, eds. *Japan in the Muromachi Age*. Berkeley: University of California Press, 1977.

Hsu, Shu-hsi. *A New Digest of Japanese War Conduct*. Shanghai: Kelly and Walsh, Ltd., 1941, pp. 77-211.

Hyland, Judy. *In the Land of the Rising Sun*. Minneapolis: Aus-burg Publishing House, 1984.

Jones, Francis C. *Japan's New Order in Asia: Its Rise and Fall, 1937-45*. London: Oxford University Press, issued under joint auspices of the Royal Institute of International Affairs and the Institute of Pacific Relations, 1954.

Ind, Colonel Allison. *Allied Intelligence Bureau: Our Secret Weapon in the War Against Japan*. New York: David McKay Company, 1958, pp. 155-56, 183-86, 272, 284.

Kahin, George McTurnan. *Nationalism and Revolution in Indonesia*. Ithaca: Cornell University Press, 1952.

Kanahele, George Sanford. "The Japanese Occupation of Indonesia: Prelude to Independence." Ph.D. Thesis. Ithaca: Cornell University, 1967.

Maass, Walter B. *The Netherlands at War: 1940-45*. London: AbelardSchuman, 1970.

Mitchell, Richard H. *Thought Control in Prewar Japan*. Ithaca: Cornell University Press, 1976.

Mook, Hubertus J. Van. *The Netherlands Indies and Japan: Their Relations 1940-41*. London: G. Allen, 1944.

Nishijima, Shigetada. *The Nishijima Collection, Materials on the Japanese Military Administration in Indonesia.* Tokyo: Institute of Social Sciences, Waseda University, 1973.

Noma, Hiroshi. *Zone of Emptiness.* Translated from French by Bernard Frechtman; translation from Japanese into French edited by Henriette de Boissel. Cleveland: The World Publishing Company, 1956.

Ooka, Shohei. *Fires on the Plain.* Translated by Ivan Morris. New York: Alfred A. Knopf, 1957.

Pritchard, R. John and Zaide, Sonia, eds. *International Military Tribunal for the Far East: The Tokyo War Crimes Trial, 1946-48.* Vol. 6. New York: Garland Publishing Inc., 1981.

Pritchard, R. John and Zaide, Sonia, eds. *International Military Tribunal for the Far East: The Tokyo War Crimes Trial, 1946-48, Index and Guide.* Vol. 3. New York: Garland Publishing Inc., 1985.

Russell of Liverpool, Lord Edvark Frederick Langby. *The Knights of Bushido: The Shocking History of the Japanese War Atrocities.* New York: E. P. Dutton and Company, Inc., 1958.

Seth, Ronald. *Secret Servants, A History of Japanese Espionage.* New York: Farrar, Straus, and Cudahy, 1957.

Sleeman, Colin and Silkin, S. C, eds. *Trial of Sumida Haruzo and Twenty Others.* War Crimes Trials Series, vol. 8. London: William Hodge and Company Ltd., 1951.

Tokayer, Marvin and Swartz, Mary. *The Fugu Plan: The Untold Story of the Japanese and the Jews During World War II.* New York: Paddington Press Ltd., 1979, pp. 226-33.

Tolischus, Otto David. *Tokyo Record.* London: Hamish Hamilton, 1943, pp. 233-46.

Van Oosten, F. C. *The Battle of the Java Sea*. Annapolis: Naval Institute Press, 1976.

Ward, Robert S. "Keepers of Public Order." In *Asia for the Asiatics? The Techniques of Japanese Occupation*, by Robert S. Ward, pp. 70-82. Chicago: Chicago University Press, 1945 (Hong Kong.)

Washington, D.C. National Archives. Record Group 226. Records of the Office of Strategic Services. On Kenpeitai in the Netherlands East Indies, see OSS Reports Nos. 98023, 13057, 21418, 117298, 117398.

Washington, D.C. National Archives. Record Group 331. Records of the Supreme Commander for the Allied Powers (SCAP).

Washington, D.C. National Archives. Record Group 389. Records of the Office of the Provost Marshall General. Prisoner of War Operations Division. Subject file, 1942-45. Japanese POW Information Bureau File.

Dutch

Brugmans, Prof. Dr. I. J.; De Graaf, Dr. H. J.; Joustra, A. H.; and Vromans, A. G. *Nederlandsch-Indie onder Japanse Bezetting, Gegevens en documenten over de jaren 1942-45*. Franeker: Uitgave T. Wever, 1960.

Velden, Doetje van. *De Japanse interneringkampen voor burgers gedurende de Tweede Wereldoorlog*. Franeker: T. Wever, 1977. Includes summary and regulations in English.

Japanese

Chōsen Kenpeitai Shireibu. *Chōsen Kenpeitai Shireibu*. Seoul: Chōsen Kenpeitai Shireibu, 1924. (Korea.)

_____. *Chōsen Kenpeitai Shireibu*. Seoul: Chōsen Kenpeitai Shireibu, 1925.

Hasegawa, Hōki. *Sumatora Mushuku.* Tokyo: Genbunsha, 1982. (Sumatra.)

Hiraki, Isamu. *Seishin Kenpei Buntai.* Yokohama: Hiraki Isamu, 1982.

Hoshjna Tokuzō. *Kenpei no Tōkon Fumetsu no Honoo: Futōmei na Sensōsaiban.* Yamagata Prefecture: Hoshina Tokuzō, 1982.

Inoue, Genkichi. *Senchi Kenpei.* Tokyo: Tosho Shuppansha, 1980.

Keijō Kenpei Buntai Kaikoroku Hensan linkai. *Pekin Keijōtai no kaikoroku.* Kurihashi-cho, Japan: Keijō Kenpei Buntai Kaikoroku Hensan linkai, 1983. (China.)

Kenpei Shireibu. *Nihon Kenpei Shōwashi.* Tokyo: Kyokutō Kenkyūsho Shuppankai, 1970.

Kenpei Shireibu. *Nihon Kenpei Shōwashi.* Tokyo: Hara Shobō, 1978.

Kobayashi, Hidezumi. *Hayashi Hidezumishi danwa Sokkiroku.* Tokyo: Kido Nikki Kenyūkai, 1976.

Kokusho Kankōkai. *Kenpei Shiberia Shuppei Kenpeishi.* Tokyo: Kokusho Kankōkai, 1976. (Siberia.)

Miyazaki, Kiyotaka. *Kenpei.* Tokyo: Fuji Shobō, 1952.

_____. *Gunpō Kaigi.* Tokyo: Fuji Shobō. 1953.

_____. *Kenpei, Gunpō kaigi.* Tokyo: Miyakawa Shobō, 1967.

Nakayama, Tokushirō. *Shiki Honkon no Seikansha.* Yokohama: Nakayama Tokushirō, 1978. (Hong Kong.)

Ōtani, Keijirō. *Kenpei Hiroku.* Tokyo: Hara Shobō, 1968.

_____. *Kenpei: Jidenteki Kaisō.* Tokyo: Shinjinbutsu Ōraisha, 1973.

———. *Shōwa Kenpeishi*. Tokyo: Misuzu Shobō, 1966. 2nd ed., Tokyo: Misuzu Shobō, 1979.

Ranan Kenyūkai. *Ranan Kenpeitai*. n.p., 1981. (Korea.)

Suzuki, Takushirō. *Kenpei Yoroku*. Tokyo: Tosho Shuppankai, 1984.

Taiwan Kenpeitaishi. *Taiwan Kenpeitai Kenyūkai*. Tokyo: Ryūkei Shosha, 1978.

Tazaki, Haruhisa. *Nihon no Kenpeitai*. Tokyo: Hara Shobō, 1971.

Tokyo Kenyukai and Zenkoku Kenyūkai Rengōkai, eds. *Junkoku Kenpei no Isho*. Tokyo: Tokyo Kenyūkai. 1982.

Tsubaki, Eiji. *Kangun Gohō no Onitachi: Aru Hojo Kenpei no Shōgen*. Tokyo: Genbunsha, 1982.

Yamada, Sadamu. *Kenpei Nikki*. Tokyo: Shinjinbutsu Ōraisha, 1982. (Sino-Japanese war.)

Yamazaki, Hideo. *Kantō Kenpeitai Kyōshūtai*. Tokushima: Shinkyō Kantō Kenpeitai Kyōshūtai Daisanki Dōkiseikai, 1982. (China.)

———. *Shisen*. Tokushima: Tokuyama Eikōsha, 1982.

Zenkoku Kenyūkai Rengōkai Hensan Iinkai. *Nihon Kenpei Seishi*. Tokyo: Zenkoku Kenyūkai Rengōkai Honbu, Kenbuin Shoin, 1976.

Zenkoku Kenyūkai Rengōkai Hensan Iinkai. *Nihon Kenpei Gaishi*. Tokyo: Zenkoku Kenyūkai Rengōkai Honbu, 1983.

www.ingramcontent.com/pod-product-compliance
Lightning Source LLC
Chambersburg PA
CBHW030345240426
43661CB00052B/1751